The Use of
FORENSIC
Anthropology

Robert B. Pickering
and
David C. Bachman

CRC Press
Boca Raton   New York   London   Tokyo

Library of Congress Cataloging-in-Publication Data

The use of forensic anthropology / Robert B. Pickering and David C. Bachman.
   p.   cm.
Includes bibliographical references and index.
ISBN 0-8493-8111-8
   1. Forensic anthropology. 2. Title. I. Pickering, Robert B. II. Bachman, David, C.
RA1063.47.F67   1996
614′.1—dc20

96-33308
CIP

Visit the CRC Web site at www.crcpress.com

© 1997 by CRC Press LLC

No claim to original U.S. Government works
International Standard Book Number 0-8493-8111-8
Library of Congress Card Number 96-33308
Printed in the United States of America   3 4 5 6 7 8 9 0
Printed on acid-free paper

Table of Contents

Preface   vii
The Authors   xi
Acknowledgments   xiii

1   Introduction   1

2   "Some Bones Have Been Found"   7
     Setting the Scene   8
     Scenario One   8
     Scenario Two   10
     Nine Key Points to Remember When Skeletal Remains
       are Discovered   13

3   What the Forensic Anthropologist Can
     and Cannot Do   15
     Finding a Forensic Anthropologist   15
     Sidebar — Physical Anthropology/Forensic Anthropology   16
     What the Forensic Anthropologist Can Do   17
     How to Find a Forensic Anthropologist   25
     Establishing the Ground Rules   28
     Sidebar — Letters of Agreement   32
     The Case Report   34
       Case Report Samples   36

**4   Techniques for Recovering Skeletonized
      Human Remains   45**

Equipment requirements   45
"I Think There Is a Skeleton Buried in this Field"   47
"Here's a Bone, We Have a Problem"   50
The Forensic Anthropologist and Recovery of Remains   56
Field Recovery   65
The Final Report   66
Things You Can Do to Make Recovery Easier   67

5   Ten Key Questions   69

Question #1: Is it bone?   69
Question #2: Is it human?   71
Question #3: Is it modern?   73
Sidebar — NAGPRA   77
Question #4: What bones are present?   78
Question #5: Is there more than one person present?   78
Question #6: What is the race, ethnicity, or cultural
   affiliation?   79
Question #7: What is the sex?   81
Question #8: What is the age?   86
Question #9: What is the stature?   91
Question #10: What are the individual characteristics
   of the remains?   93
Summary   96

6   Determination of Time Since Death   97

The Body   99
The Micro Environment   100
Eight Essential Environmental Categories of Information   102

**7   Special Techniques — Their Value
      and Limitations   105**

Facial Reconstruction   105
Direct Facial Reconstruction   106
Craniofacial Superimposition   110
Video Superimposition   112

Footprint Impression Analysis   112
Osteon Counting   113
Bitemark Analysis   114
ABO Blood Typing   115
Forensic Toxicology   116
^{14}C Dating   117
DNA Testing   117

**8   Skeletal Trauma and Identifying
       Skeletal Pathology   119**

Ante-Mortem Trauma   119
Peri-Mortem Trauma   122
Post-Mortem Trauma   124
Pseudo-Trauma   130
Pathologic Changes in Bone   131
Follow-Up Steps for Skeletal Abnormalities   138

9   Putting Your Case Together   139

Closing the Case, Closing the Book   141

Bibliography   145

Glossary   147

Appendix: Report Forms   153

Human Remains Investigation:
    Cover Sheet   154
    Forensic Anthropology Summary   155
    General Information   157
    Contextual Description   158
    Recovery Area   159
    General Description of Remains   160
    Inventory   162
    Photo and Video Inventory   163

Index   165

Preface

This book is written for medical examiners, coroners, and other law enforcement officers who are responsible for conducting death investigations. Forensic analysis has become and will continue to be a complex and highly specialized field of study. No longer can the lone investigator take on the responsibilities of doing all the work of recovery, examination, and interpretation of a human remains resulting from unexplained circumstances. Today, a forensic investigation requires a team of specialists from many different scientific fields of study as well as legal and law enforcement specialists.

Of the many specialties that sometimes are used in forensic investigation, forensic anthropology is most often associated with the analysis of skeletonized human remains. While this characterization is correct, it also is true that in recent years the range of cases on which forensic anthropologists consult has expanded dramatically. Unfortunately, forensic anthropology has become a popular topic for novels, TV programs, and even movies. While publicity sometimes can be helpful, the wrong kind of publicity can raise expectations beyond what the real specialist is able to deliver. Moreover, frequent publicity in the media about forensic anthropologists make it appear that these specialists are more numerous than they really are.

This volume is written to give the medicolegal officer some guidelines for determining how to choose and when to use a forensic anthropologist. This book assumes that the medicolegal officer is not a trained anthropologist and is not particularly interested in how anthropologists do what they do. As Andy Principe, founder and former Director of the Northern Illinois Police Crime Lab once said, "Bob, cops don't give a damn about how you do your job. They want to know how you are going to help them do their job." The authors assume that you want to do your job effectively and efficiently. This book shows how forensic anthropologists can help you do a better job.

The authors have tried to write this volume in a manner that is enjoyable to read as well as informative. Many examples and anecdotes are offered to illustrate the theoretical and procedural points that we are trying to make. We have tried to keep in mind that you are not necessarily anthropological or medical specialists. For that reason, we have kept jargon to a minimum to make our writing as clear as possible. Unfortunately, it is impossible to eliminate all jargon; indeed, jargon is the language each group of specialists invents to talk among themselves about their subject. To the best of our abilities, the authors will define terms in context so that a common use and understanding can be achieved.

Chapter 1 introduces the field of forensic anthropology. A historical overview shows that, in one form or another, forensic anthropology has been around for at least two hundred years. Frequently, forensic anthropology has been associated with the recovery and identification of soldiers deceased in military conflicts.

Chapter 2 gives basic information about how to approach a forensic recovery site. A number of common-sense guidelines should be followed in order to maximize the retrievable information, while minimizing redundant effort and personnel. One of those suggestions pertains to who exactly is required to be on the site and when, vs. those who have come to watch. Although access is sometimes a sensitive matter, particularly when other officers or elected officials are involved, it is crucial that it be controlled.

Chapter 3 offers some insights into forensic anthropology as a discipline and how one goes about finding the right forensic anthropologist. As mentioned earlier, although it might appear that there are many forensic anthropologists available, in fact there are fewer than 70 and they are not evenly distributed across the U.S. Finding one may not always be easy. The best way to do it is in advance rather than waiting for a case to force the issue.

Chapter 4 discusses some of the scenarios in which the forensic anthropologist is helpful. A point repeatedly stressed is that the analysis and interpretation begins at the recovery site. If at all possible, the anthropologist should be part of the recovery team. The sooner he or she enters the case, the more comprehensive and better the data that will result. Forensic anthropologists, particularly those also trained in archaeology, can be invaluable. One of the old stereotypes of anthropologists is that they take too long to excavate. Just the opposite is true. Because these people have the knowledge of and experience with human remains and excavation techniques, they can excavate faster, more efficiently, and more carefully than people without training.

Once the recovery is made, detailed analysis begins. Chapter 5 presents a series of ten questions that need to be answered about each case. Each is illustrated by real cases. This chapter also stresses that there is an order to the ten questions. The answers to early ones are necessary for the accurate determination of the later ones.

Chapter 6 discusses one of the most difficult variables: determination of time since death. Many factors relating to the body and environment affect this variable. Understanding the kinds of changes that are important makes it easier to understand that this variable is best given and estimated as a time range.

Like every other science, forensic investigation now includes techniques that did not exist a decade ago. Chapter 7 discusses some of the most important of these techniques. This chapter stresses that each technique has value but also limitations. No technique, regardless of how good or promising, works in all cases. Good use of scientific techniques includes recognizing the limits of each technique.

Chapter 8 is an overview of the major categories of trauma — ante-mortem, peri-mortem, and post-mortem — that may be observed in forensic cases. Each has a story to tell but not all of them relate to cause and manner of death. In fact, it is important to know how to differentiate between those incidences of trauma that occurred around the time of death and those that did not. Similarly, evidence of pathology on the skeleton also can be a valuable aid to identification, if properly identified.

Chapter 9 brings the various parts of the process together to reconstruct a case. Again, the point of this book is not to make the reader a professional forensic anthropologist but rather to define how an anthropologist can help an investigation, and perhaps more importantly, to instruct the reader on how to locate one.

Finally, the forms, glossary, and lists of contacts will provide specific tools and information to help the medicolegal officer create a system and a group of consultants that will contribute to the resolution of cases.

We had five goals when writing this book: first, to help you develop a standard protocol to follow when investigating skeletal remains; second, to remind you what kinds of questions you must have answered in such a case; third, to tell you who the people are who can provide those answers; fourth, to give you some direction on finding those experts; and fifth, to explain some of the steps the experts follow in trying to learn the answers to your questions. We want this book to serve as a guide for the law enforcement officer who is the first responder to a scene with skeletal remains and for the investigators from every agency who are responsible for solving the puzzle of the who, when, and how of an unexplained death.

The Authors

Robert B. Pickering, Ph.D., has been Chairman of the Anthropology Department and Curator of Anthropology at the Denver Museum of Natural History since 1991. He is also an Associate Professor Adjunct in the Anthropology Department, University of Colorado at Denver. Pickering serves as an anthropological consultant to various Coroners in Colorado and is a member of the National Disaster Medical System (NDMS) Disaster Mortuary Team (DMORT), District VIII.

Dr. Pickering received his Ph.D. in Physical Anthropology from Northwestern University in 1984. He received a B.A. and M.A. in anthropology from Southern Illinois University in 1972 and 1973, respectively.

Dr. Pickering was presented with the Forensic Service Award from the Royal Thai Institute of Forensic Medicine in Bangkok in 1994 and a Service Award from the Fourth Indo-Pacific Congress on Legal Medicine and Forensic Sciences in 1992. Pickering was elected to Sigma Xi in 1989 and received a Letter of Commendation from the Commander of the U.S. Army Central Identification Laboratory in Hawaii in 1976.

Dr. Pickering is a Fellow of the Anthropology Section of the American Academy of Forensic Sciences and a member of the American Association of Physical Anthropologists, the Paleopathology Association, and the Society for American Archaeology. In the past six years, Pickering has served as a grant reviewer for the National Endowment of the Humanities and the Wenner-Gren Foundation.

Since 1990, Pickering has presented 17 papers, written 12 articles, written 2 children's books on archaeology, and edited 12 children's books on anthropology.

David C. Bachman, M.D., graduated from Northwestern University Medical School in 1962 and completed his residency in Orthopedic Surgery in the Northwestern Orthopedic Program in 1967. He began private practice and served as Assistant Professor of Orthopedic Surgery at Northwestern until 1980. During that time he also served as Director of the Center for Sports Medicine at Northwestern and as team physician for the Chicago Bulls.

In 1980, he moved to Ouray County, Colorado, where he continued private practice and was elected coroner of Ouray County; he also served as Chairman of the County Emergency Management Board. In 1993, after retiring from private practice, he moved to Denver, Colorado, and now is a medical consultant for the U.S. Post Office. He is also a Research Associate in the Department of Anthropology at the Denver Museum of Natural History.

Publications include a syndicated sports medicine newspaper column from 1978–1991 and three books which he has co-written: *Dear Dr. Jock, The People's Guide to Sports and Fitness*; *The Diet that Let's you Cheat*; and *The Way it Was*.

Acknowledgments

We owe a special debt of thanks to many people. Triena Harper, Chief Deputy Coroner, Jefferson County, CO provided photos, editorial comments, and support as we worked our way to completion of this book. James Quale, M.D., orthopedic radiologist, Swedish Medical Center, Englewood, CO, graciously opened his teaching file to provide X-rays of some unique skeletal problems. Linda Shulzkump, M.D., created all of the line drawings in the text and collaborated on how best to present their content. Rick Wicker, photographer for the Denver Museum of Natural History, shot some of the photos that were needed to illustrate certain points. Lynne Bachman Brown did the initial editing of our manuscript, cleaning up the errors in grammar, punctuation, and syntax. JoAnn Fox, Office Manager of the Anthropology Department, was a great help in organizing drafts of manuscripts, formatting, and all of the time-consuming tasks that are needed to turn a manuscript into a book. To all of our colleagues who loaned us slides for the book, critiqued our concept, and helped us work through various points, we thank you very much. To the extent that this book is successful, all of you deserve some credit. For any errors, we take responsibility.

Finally, we owe a debt of gratitude to Joel Claypod for his early encouragement when we proposed this project and to Helen Linna, our editor at CRC Press, who labored so diligently to bring it to completion.

Introduction

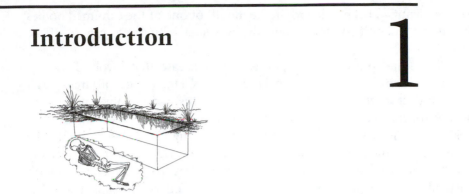

Forensic anthropology has a long tradition in the United States. Its roots are intertwined with other medical and scientific disciplines such as human anatomy, paleontology, dentistry, archaeology, and anthropology. As is true for many kinds of technical and medical developments, the history and use of forensic anthropology is closely linked to military action.

T. Dale Stewart, himself one of the most significant American forensic anthropologists, considers Thomas Dwight, M.D., to be the father of American forensic anthropology. Dwight's first paper was published in 1878 and was called *The Identification of Human Skeleton, A Medicolegal Study*. Dwight then went on to conduct important research and to publish extensively on topics in human anatomy and forensic anthropology.

More than 10 years earlier during the Civil War, the Union forces began an organized approach to the recovery of the remains of soldiers fallen in battle. The Graves Registration mission of recovering and burying the dead was given to the Quartermaster Corps. Some efforts were made to identify individuals but success was based almost solely on presence of personal effects.

Surprisingly, there are two important cases that used the methods of forensic anthropology even before the Civil War. During the American Revolution, Dr. Joseph Warren was a medical doctor and an officer in the Continental Army. In 1775, he was killed at the Battle of Bunker Hill and his body was buried by the British with that of another American solider in an unmarked grave. More than a year later the two remains were exhumed. At this point, another important historic figure enters the picture. When he was not riding around at midnight or smithing silver table services for wealthy families, Paul Revere made dentures. In fact, he had made a set of dentures out of "hyppotomus" teeth and silver wire for the deceased Dr. Warren.

Revere identified his handiwork in the mouth of one of the exhumed bodies and thereby identified Dr. Warren who was later reburied as a hero of the revolution.

The second pre-Civil War case is a civilian case that involved money, power, and some fine old New England families. Dr. George Parkman was a medical doctor who, after retirement, focused his considerable energies on his investments. He rented small houses in the poorer sections of Boston and personally made the rounds collecting rent. Although he begins to sound like a soulmate of the Dickens character Ebenezer Scrooge, Parkman had many good points. He was an important donor to Harvard University and took particular interest in its Massachusetts Medical College. Perhaps it was this interest that led him to lend money to Dr. John White Webster, one of the professors at the college.

Although from a powerful and important family himself, Dr. Webster found that the Harvard salary did not allow him to indulge his expensive tastes. He also had two unmarried daughters to worry about. Within a few years, he was in debt to Dr. Parkman for thousands of dollars. Things began to get ugly when Parkman found out that Webster had used a mineral collection as collateral to another creditor; unfortunately, that same collection was already mortgaged to Parkman. After about 1:00 p.m. on the afternoon of Friday, November 23, 1849, Dr. Parkman was never seen alive again.

When an important man is missing, things happen fast. In this case, the circumstances and the trail seemed to lead to Dr. Webster, who taught anatomy at the college. Having portions of remains around and having to dispose of remains were common practices in his lab. However, the police and the public were shocked to hear that some of the fragments found in an incinerator appeared to belong to the missing Dr. Parkman. With the testimony of Dr. Parkman's dentist and other medical experts, Dr. Webster was convicted of the crime. Before he was hanged, he admitted his guilt and sought both forgiveness and redemption. His body was buried in an unmarked grave, its location known to a few of Webster's close associates but not to his family for fear that his notoriety would attract ghouls and body snatchers.

As mentioned earlier, forensic anthropology begins to take on a more systematic and rigorous nature with the work of Thomas Dwight. By the end of the 19th and the beginning of the 20th century, however, another important person, George A. Dorsey, appeared on the scene. In many ways George Dorsey represented the best of the early field of anthropology. He conducted ethnographic fieldwork among various Plains Indian tribes before 1900 and published his work through the Field Museum of Natural History in Chicago; his early descriptions are still valued today. Dorsey believed in popularizing anthropology and wrote a number of books that made anthropology intelligible and interesting to the public. He could conduct research and make it interesting to nonspecialists. Frankly, one of the reasons this book has been written is that George Dorsey's anthropological life is a model of professionalism for one of the authors (RBP).

In addition to his academic anthropology, George Dorsey was involved in investigating a number of criminal cases in Chicago, the most famous being the Luetgert case. Luetgert, a sausage maker, decided to dispose of his troublesome wife in one of the sausage vats. He nearly succeeded; however, it appears that attention to detail and neatness were not two of Luetgert's strong points. In the bottom of a vat from which caustic fumes rose, investigators found small pieces of bone as well as Mrs. Luetgert's wedding ring. Although medical specialists said that none of the bones were identifiable as human, Dr. Dorsey convinced the jury that they were. His statement marks the first time that the testimony of a physical anthropologist was given more weight than that of a medical doctor, and Luetgert was eventually convicted of murdering his wife. Interestingly, this was Dorsey's last case; within a few years, he left anthropology altogether and went into military service during World War I.

During the 1920s, T.W. Todd, an anatomist, was beginning to look at large series of human skeletons and finding regularities in the age changes that occur on various parts of the skeleton. Perhaps his greatest contribution was the recognition that the pubic symphysis goes through regular changes and is an important indicator of age.

Dr. Todd was a teacher of another important contributor to forensic anthropology, Wilton Marion Krogman. His article on the identification of skeletal remains, published in the *FBI Law Enforcement Bulletin*, is the beginning of the modern era in forensic anthropology, according to Stewart. Besides the many people Krogman introduced to and mentored in forensic work, perhaps his most lasting contribution is the book, *The Human Skeleton in Forensic Medicine*, the first book to focus on forensic anthropology.

During Krogman's long and productive professional life, he saw forensic anthropology change from a scientific novelty into a mature discipline. Researchers in universities and medical schools were developing new information about skeletons and techniques for determining biological characteristics such as sex, age, stature, and race and the results were being applied in both civilian and military settings.

World War II was responsible for the next great advance in forensic knowledge. Sadly, like all forensic work, it was a response to a great need. In both the European and Pacific theaters of the War many soldiers were dying and, at times, their bodies were not immediately recoverable. In the Pacific, because of the heat and humidity, bodies could be reduced to skeletons in days rather than weeks or months. In 1947, the U.S. Army opened the first Central Identification Laboratory (CIL) at a military mortuary facility in

Hawaii. Dr. Charles Snow from the University of Kentucky was the Army's first "physical" anthropologist as the term "forensic" anthropologist had not come into use at this time.

Eventually, Dr. Mildred Trotter, Professor of Gross Anatomy at Washington University in St. Louis, also went to the CIL facility in Hawaii. Like Snow, she was interested not just in identifying the military dead but also using the experience to gain greater knowledge of the human skeleton, patterns of age change, and post-mortem changes in the body due to decomposition. Trotter, in particular, recognized that in addition to serving her country by helping to identify the war dead, she also needed to use this extraordinary opportunity to examine large numbers of skeletons from the military sector to develop better methods of analysis for future generations. The work of these fine scholars is still used today. They began asking the questions that present day forensic anthropologists are still researching.

During the Korean War, employing physical anthropologists to identify the war dead was no longer an experiment, but a standard. At various times, throughout the war and after, T. Dale Stewart, Thomas W. McKern, Ellis Kerley, and Charles P. Warren worked as physical anthropologists for the Army. The most valuable anthropological result of this work was McKern and Stewart's *Skeletal Age Changes in Young American Males*. This important work is still a standard and has led to the development of many additional researches into skeletal changes associated with age, sex, and race.

Following the Korean War, Stewart returned to his post at the Smithsonian and was active in forensic and archaeological research for the rest of his professional career. McKern returned to teaching. Much later, both Kerley and Warren returned to government service as a result of the Vietnam War. Warren had been in the University of the Philippines in 1950–1951 on a Fulbright scholarship when he was called to come to Japan. Previously, he had received a B.S. degree in zoology from Northwestern University and was the Big Ten's first African-American varsity quarterback. Before going to the Philippines, he received an M.A. in anthropology at Indiana University. Warren served as a physical anthropologist in Japan until 1955 and then returned to Chicago to teach at the Navy Pier campus, which eventually was renamed the University of Illinois at Chicago and was moved to another part of the city. Chuck Warren moved with the university as part of the anthropology faculty. At the time of his death, he had more years of service to the university than any other anthropology faculty member. From 1973–1975, Warren was on leave from the university while again working as a physical anthropologist at the U.S. Army Central Identification Laboratory in Thailand. Warren's contribution to research includes work on the effects of tropical plant growth as an agent of decomposition and study of the social dynamics of the CIL.

Ellis Kerley returned to university teaching after his stint in Korea. For many years, he conducted research in human osteology using both forensic and archaeologically recovered samples. One of his most important contributions was developing the technique of osteon counting to determine age (see Chapter 7 for more about this). In 1976, the Army's CIL lab moved from Thailand to Hawaii. In 1987, Kerley returned to the CIL lab and became the Chief of the Anthropology Laboratory.

Overlapping the time of Warren and Kerley were two other anthropologists. Tadao Furue worked for the U.S. Army in Japan and served as physical anthropologist from the mid-1950s until 1977, at which time he and his family immigrated to Hawaii where Furue became the CIL's anthropologist. Furue experimented with many identification techniques. One of the most promising was the craniofacial superimposition technique (see Chapter 7 for more information). Tadao Furue served the U.S. government as an anthropologist until his death in 1988.

In 1975–1976, one of the authors of this book, Bob Pickering, was the physical anthropologist at the CIL in Thailand and during its transition to Hawaii. After his one-year tour of duty, Pickering went to Northwestern, finished the Ph.D. program in physical anthropology in 1984, and has been consulting in forensic work since that time.

Today, the U.S. Army CIL fields the largest forensic team in the world. In addition to the military recovery and support staff, there are ten physical anthropologists and three odontologists who work together to recover and identify remains not only from Southeast Asia, but also from the Korean War and various sites of World War II battles. The mission of the CIL also includes the recovery and analysis of recent military disasters such as the Gander Mountain plane crash. Over the years it has become one of the premier forensic facilities in the world.

As can be seen from the preceding discussion, the American military has recognized the importance of physical anthropology to the identification of human remains for over half a century. In the civilian sector, however, formal recognition is not so old. Before 1971, Wilton Krogman was the only member of the Anthropology section of the American Academy of Forensic Sciences, an organization of professional forensic specialists. In 1972 the Physical Anthropology section of the academy was founded. However, from that relatively recent beginning, the section has grown dramatically. More important than the numbers, forensic anthropology is now considered to be an integral part of forensic investigation.

"Some Bones Have Been Found"

2

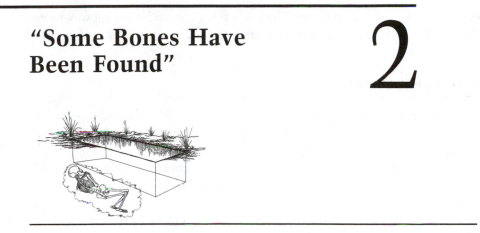

All of us with responsibility for investigating death scenes have developed a standard procedure to ensure that our investigation is thorough and complete. We have perfected this technique through experience and training and try to follow it on every case.

There is one circumstance where that standard approach does not always meet our needs. This happens when we encounter a bunch of bones or a decomposing carcass rather than the expected recently dead body. Most of us rarely encounter this problem and most of us lack training in recovery of skeletal remains. Because of that we cannot rely on our standard procedure and, worse, our investigation runs the risk of being compromised.

Badly decomposed remains have lost several of the components that we rely on for identification such as facial features, fingerprints, and body weight. Fully skeletonized remains have lost eye and hair color. Disarticulated remains make estimation of stature difficult. Burned remains make everything seem impossible.

A number of other things complicate our investigation, some under our control but most are not. Things that you cannot control include destruction of the remains by the perpetrator, animals, or time. Lack of personal effects or artifacts and absence of any unique skeletal characteristic make identification of the subject difficult, if not impossible.

Loss of these components makes the question of who this person was and when and how he or she died more difficult to answer. This is the time when we may need some outside help to find those answers.

Regardless of the state in which the remains are found, the one thing you do control, and the element that may have the greatest effect on your ability to solve this puzzle of who this person is and how death occurred, is how you conduct your investigation. There is a right way and a wrong way to do things. This chapter describes two scenarios that demonstrate these two ways.

Setting the Scene

"Hello Sheriff, this is John Brown and I think I just found a body. I was out hunting and I came across what looks like a human skeleton in the woods."

Great, what do you do now? Well, this is hunting season and chances are this isn't an April Fool's joke. Your first step is to contact someone from the coroner's office to go with you to meet John Brown and have a look at this body.

John Brown is right, this looks like a human skeleton to you, too. So what's your next step? It is November, it is 6:00 p.m., there's snow on the ground, and the temperature is 5°F. If you're smart, you won't make the same mistake one coroner did with his first skeletal remains case.

Scenario One

It was a Sunday night and the dispatcher called to report the discovery of a body on the side of the mountain south of town. The rest of the scenario was the same: night, snow, and cold. A couple of sheriff's deputies, an EMT, and the coroner accompanied the reporting party to the scene which was about a quarter of a mile off a county road. It was a body of a white male, dressed in khaki Army surplus clothes lying on a rocky ledge next to a large pine tree. They could see the body was male as it had a red beard, but that was about all they could tell. The body had been there for some time and birds and animals had done their work. The eyes were gone along with all the abdominal organs. The skin of the exposed hands and bare feet was decomposed past the point at which fingerprinting was possible. Because the body was lying on a south-facing slope the sun had desiccated the skin of the face to the point that it appeared mummified.

So what did they do? They used their flashlights to look around and discovered an old knapsack, a few canned food items, a pair of hiking boots with socks, and an old blanket stored under the low-hanging limbs of the pine tree. It was obvious that the man had been camping there for a while. Then, they made their first serious error by putting the body in a body bag, heading back to town, and transporting the body to the morgue. They did one thing right though, they ordered an autopsy. But did they do anything else right that night? Did they take photos? Did they really examine the scene with the body in place to see if they could figure out what happened? Did a scene investigation give them any clues about who this man was? No, it was cold, it was dark, they had other plans. They hustled the body away before a real investigation could be done. Why? Was the body going to get up and leave town that night? Was someone going to steal it? Not likely. They disobeyed the first rule of forensic investigation: *don't move the body until your investigation is complete.*

This situation, as all cases of discovered skeletal remains, required a full forensic investigation. This was a homicide until proven otherwise. There were many unanswered questions. Who was this man? How did he get here? How long had he been here? How did he die?

At the morgue they searched the body and clothing and found nothing helpful. There was no identification, no wallet, and just a few coins in the pants pocket. He wore no jewelry. There were no name tags in the clothing. An inventory of the body did not reveal any external evidence of gunshot or stab wounds and no signs of major skull trauma. They had to wait for a formal autopsy report to see if they could learn the cause of death.

The next day they returned to the scene to collect the remaining belongings and to search the area for other clues. The knapsack gave no information. There were no letters with a name. The other clothing had no name tags. The hiking shoes were worn and of a common type. Nothing was found that offered a clue to this man's identity.

The autopsy gave more information: the man's age was estimated to be about 40 years old, he was approximately 6 feet tall, and probably weighed about 150 pounds. That was the best possible estimate because of the advanced decomposition. What was his eye color? Unknown; they were gone. The pathologist's estimate of the time of death was several weeks earlier based on the soft tissue preservation and the winter conditions present at the site. The fact that the body was lying on a rocky ledge with full daily sun exposure made that estimate inexact. The dental exam revealed a full set of teeth with some fillings. That gave hope that information existed somewhere that would identify this man.

X-rays showed no evidence of long bone fractures. No bullet fragments were found on X-ray and there was no evidence of chest wounds found on autopsy. There was a small, 0.5 in. laceration on the back of the scalp. X-rays of the skull revealed a linear fracture in the occiput. Had this man been struck on the head and murdered? That was not probable. A blow on the head from a blunt instrument that kills someone produces a skull fracture similar to what you see when you crack a hard-boiled egg. The point of impact is usually crushed in and fracture lines radiate from that impact point in all directions. A linear skull fracture is usually caused by the body falling with the head hitting a hard surface. The pathologist did not think that his skull fracture was enough to kill this man. So what was the cause of death? The best they could come up with was a probable cause. It looked as if he had fallen and struck his head hard enough to knock himself unconscious. As he was lightly dressed, lying outside in the mountains in the winter, the probable cause of death was hypothermia; the manner of death was accidental, not a homicide or suicide.

With that information the investigation continued. Interviewers in town asked if any one had seen a 6-foot, 150-pound, bearded, redheaded white male about 40 years old dressed in army-surplus khaki clothing in the past few weeks. One of the clerks at the local market vaguely remembered some-one of that description buying food in the past but had no idea who he might be. No one else had any recollection of anyone of that description. Dental X-rays were shown to the 18 dentists in the surrounding area; there was no match. There were no missing persons reports that matched the man's description. One of the nearby counties had been searching for a missing hunter for several weeks, but this man did not fit their missing man's description.

What did they know? They had an unidentified man who had probably died of hypothermia several weeks ago. There were many questions they were unable to answer. What were the circumstances that lead to his death? Had he been alone? Was there any evidence that someone else had been with him? They certainly could not answer that. They had trampled all over the scene in the dark peering under the tree with flashlights and removing the body. Any tracks that might have been present had been totally obscured by their conduct. Had he been stabbed in the abdomen by some unknown assailant? No one could tell that because the abdominal organs were absent. Was there any sign of blood on the ground? As a matter of fact there was a small amount. After they learned that there was a small scalp laceration they went back to the scene and found some blood on a small rock that appeared to be where they thought his head was lying when he was discovered, but they didn't know this for sure because they had moved him in the dark.

This was a straightforward case of discovered remains of a recently deceased man. They could guess that he was a lone transient who had hiked to the site to set up a campsite for the night. Moisture on the rocks probably caused him to slip and fall, striking his head hard enough to render him unconscious. Lying there unconscious in the cold produced hypothermia and death. They knew a good bit about him: height, probable weight, age, cloth-ing, dental records, and approximate date of death, but they were still unable to identify him.

Scenario Two

Let's return to the first case of John Brown's body. This time let's review the recovery as it should be conducted. You begin securing the site for the night, then wait until morning and return with a full team to do your investigation.

Who do you want on your team? The most experienced investigators from both local law enforcement and the coroner's office make the best team. While this case will arouse much interest in town you don't want the press as this is still a possible homicide investigation. Limit the number of people at the scene. The more people there are at the scene the more likely it is that someone will walk over and obscure some piece of evidence that is crucial to your investigation.

Before you start a more detailed examination, your first step should be to photograph the scene with the body in place and to make a map to record location details. If you end up in court, your investigation is only as good as your records so make sure they are complete.

Next, get detailed photos of the body. It is evident that you have a major problem. While this is a full skeleton, it is just that; your subject is completely skeletonized. There is no tissue on the body, no hair, nothing to indicate race or sex, and nothing to give you a hint about how long this body may have been here.

This is the time when you had better have a plan for how you are going to proceed. Because the skeletal remains can give no additional help, you will have to look elsewhere for any information that might help you resolve this situation. The first step is to search the surrounding area. It would be helpful to know that there are no other bodies lying around. Is there anything else in the area that might be helpful? An abandoned vehicle, luggage, boxes — anything out of the ordinary might provide clues. It is unlikely that tracks in the area are going to be helpful since it appears that this body has been here for a long time. Unfortunately there does not appear to be anything unusual in these woods.

After the area search is complete, it is time to look at the area immediately around the body. What are you going to look for? You would look for artifacts or anything that would not naturally occur here. You're lucky and find some bits of clothing and some decaying shoes. It looks as if the subject was wearing denim pants and a flannel shirt. The shoes seem to be remnants of hunting boots. While not certain, these clues increase the odds that this subject was a male. More men than women hunt.

That pretty much exhausts what you can learn from the skeleton at the site. Since you photographed the body from all angles earlier, now you take detailed photos of each body section before removing any portion. Next, you collect all the bones, making certain that you label each individual bone as you bag it. All of the bones, even the smallest one, may give an expert a clue about this death. Did you find the hyoid? If that is intact you can be fairly certain that your subject was not choked to death. Did you find all the small bones of the hands and feet? Has something carried them off?

After the bones are removed, it is time to sift the ground under and around the skeleton. Look for any signs of bug debris; they could help make a determination of time since death. Sift all the dirt through a ¼-in. screen. Again, you are lucky as there are some coins partly buried in the dirt next to the subject's hip. The latest coin is dated 1984. You know this is not a discovery of an ancient Native American. This subject was alive in 1984. You still don't know how or exactly when this person died. Here's a metal button that has Levi Strauss and Co. printed on it. That confirms your find of denim jeans. More sifting turns up two bullets. Your weapons expert identifies them as 30-30 bullets. Does that mean your subject has been shot? Maybe, but people have been hunting in these woods for years. All these finds are photographed, recorded, tagged, and bagged. Collect *everything* you find at the scene. If it turns out to be unimportant when it is examined in the lab you can throw it away without causing any problems. The problem arises when you ignore something at the scene that may be important. Going back and finding it later may be impossible.

What do you know so far? You have skeletal remains of a subject, possibly male, that died sometime in 1984 or after and who may have been shot. Is there anything else you can learn at the site? Probably not. You've done your part thoroughly and that is about all you can do. You're going to need professional help to tell you more about this skeleton. Your medical examiner will look at the skeleton but will probably need to call in a forensic anthropologist to help unravel your problem. What can this person tell you? The anthropologist will be able to provide you with the subject's sex, an age in a fairly limited range, the stature, and race. That will help you narrow the investigation as you search missing persons records. A forensic anthropologist also may be able to identify skeletal damage caused by a knife or bullet; information that is essential for determining cause and manner of death.

In this situation, the initial investigation of John Brown's body was straightforward. But what if you had found just a few scattered bones at the scene? How should you handle that situation? Are you or anyone in your department expert in identifying bones? Are you sure these bones are human? Do you know if you have a complete skeleton scattered around, or just a part of a skeleton? Worse, do you have parts of several skeletons? If it is just part of a skeleton, were these bones dug up by animals with the rest of the skeleton in a grave near by? Could you find the grave? Or did some homicidal fiend dismember another person and scatter different body parts all over the county? Are you able to recognize cremated remains? If you're smart you will protect the scene and go for help. The most expert help in a situation like this is a forensic anthropologist — someone experienced in finding and examining skeletal remains that may form part of a crime scene.

Nine Key Points To Remember When Skeletal Remains Are Discovered

1. Do a full investigation, this is a homicide until proven otherwise.
2. Establish a plan before you begin.
3. Get your key people to the scene for the investigation.
4. Don't move the remains until you have completed a thorough investigation; there is no rush.
5. Search the area for artifacts and clues.
6. Collect and tag all the bones and all objects.
7. Sift the ground under and around the remains.
8. Make sure your report is complete and accurate; this includes photographs and mapping.
9. Get expert help if you still have unanswered questions.

What the Forensic Anthropologist Can and Cannot Do

3

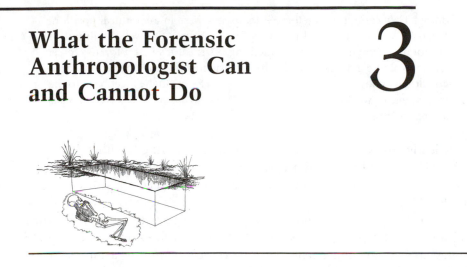

Finding a Forensic Anthropologist

The forensic anthropologist is one of the specialists who can greatly contribute to the collection and analysis of evidence in a case. At minimum, the forensic anthropologist can determine the major biological characteristics such as age, sex, stature, and possibly race of a skeletonized human remains. However, forensic anthropologists often can do much more than collect evidence in a wide range of cases. Because of their training, forensic anthropologists may help reconstruct the events that led to the crime scene and may provide a sharply focused image of the deceased. The first step toward taking advantage of the anthropologist's abilities is to find one and begin developing a working relationship before the first case.

The following scenario is fictitious; unfortunately, it also is rather common. It typifies the kind of misunderstanding that can occur without finding a consulting anthropologist before you actually need one.

> Some bones are found out in the woods. The medicolegal officer, thinks the bones are probably human, but doesn't know for certain. The officer takes them to the nearest college campus and asks for someone who knows about bones. Once the contact is made, the officer brings the bag of bones over to the "professor" and says, "Well, Doc, tell me all you can." After ascertaining that there are no photos or field notes, the professor rather anxiously peers into the bag of dirty broken bones and says, "I'll get back to you in a few weeks." The professor is thinking: "These guys don't know what they're

doing! They cannot even tell me if the bones were in anatomical position. I don't have any time until the end of the semester. Oh well, I will put in an hour or two and tell them something. After all it's **just** a forensic case; it's not real research." Meanwhile the forensic investigator is thinking: "This guy doesn't know what he's doing! What does he mean, he'll get back to me in a couple of weeks. Doesn't he realize this case has to be resolved? This is a forensic case, not some crazy research project!"

Clearly, this kind of interaction is neither satisfying to either party nor is it likely to produce the most detailed evidence. Unfortunately, virtually every forensic anthropologist and probably most medicolegal officers have a similar story. It is based on a number of faulty assumptions on both sides. First, not all physical anthropologists, and very few archaeologists, are trained as forensic anthropologists. Because of that lack of forensic perspective, the professor may not understand the importance of time in a forensic case. Because of the lack of background information, the anthropologist's report may either be too short or too tentative. Conversely, a professor trained as an osteologist may provide an abundance of descriptive detail that is unreadable and unwanted by the investigating officer. Two assumptions, both faulty, are commonly found among investigators: either they think that the professor can determine only a few biological traits such as age, sex, and height or they expect that the anthropologist can determine eye color, state and county of birth, and possibly religious preference. Both of these assumptions miss the mark. Forensic anthropologists can interpret the data available. The more data, the better the interpretation. As is true when people from different fields work on the same project, communication and a common understanding are critical to success.

Physical Anthropology/Forensic Anthropology

A forensic anthropologist is a specialist in recovering and identifying human remains. As a college undergraduate, this person may have come through any one of a number of disciplines including anthropology, archaeology, criminalistics, or pre-medicine. They have had graduate training in human osteology, recovery techniques, and the analysis of human remains. While different forensic anthropologists have their own research interests, all should be able to help the forensic investigator recover, analyze, and identify remains.

A physical anthropologist studies humans as biological beings. The range of topics within this seemingly simple statement is enormous. Some physical anthropologists may focus on the morphology (size and shape) of the fossilized ancestors of modern humans or on the biology and behavior of other primates, such as chimps, gorillas, or macaques. Among the physical anthropologists who study modern humans, the subjects may range from the study of high altitude adaptations in various parts of the world to concepts of health and sickness in different cultures. Others focus more precisely on nutrition of infants and how different models of child care affect newborns. Not all physical anthropologists study human bones, just as not all medical doctors are forensic pathologists. While many forensic anthropologists begin as physical anthropologists and may continue to conduct research or teach in other areas of anthropology, the forensic investigator should not assume that any physical anthropologist is also a forensic specialist.

An archaeologist is an anthropologist who studies ancient cultures and people. While some archaeologists are trained in human osteology, many are not. An archaeologist can certainly be helpful in recovering a buried remains; however, that person may not be familiar with the kinds of questions that are important in a forensic investigation.

Anthropology is the study of human beings and their cultures. All the above specialties are part of the discipline of anthropology, which also includes linguistics, cultural anthropology, and other fields that normally are not directly relevant to forensic cases.

What the Forensic Anthropologist Can Do

Forensic anthropologists can help you recover and analyze human remains, particularly those that are decomposed or skeletonized, in a rapid, efficient manner. The training of a forensic anthropologist allows them to recover skeletons quickly. Besides rapid recovery, their training enables them to glean more information from the site that may be of value in later analysis. Once recovered, the forensic anthropologist can determine many of the biological characteristics of a skeleton that are needed to identify the deceased. Finally, the anthropologist will find any relevant clues on the bones and teeth that may be related to cause of death.

Perhaps the first question to be asked by the medicolegal officer is: "How can a forensic anthropologist help me?" To some extent that answer is defined by the case and by the specific training and experience of the forensic anthropologist. However, it is possible to outline the kinds of cases in which anthropologists have been helpful.

To make a gross generalization, there are four scenarios in which human remains require examination:

1. Complete remains with no or minimal decomposition
2. Decomposing remains

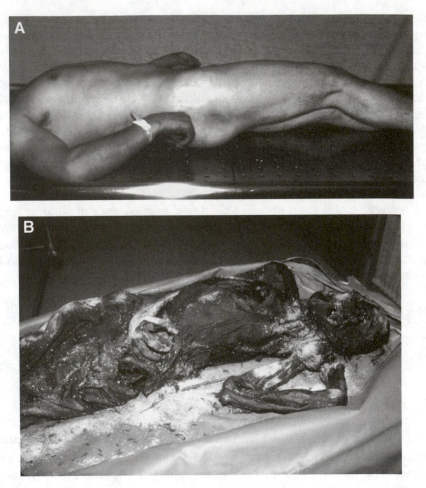

Figure 1   Four conditions of remains. The greater the decomposition, the more often a forensic anthropologist is called in the case. (A) Complete remains; (B) decomposing remains; (C) skeletal remains; and (D) cremated remains. (Photos courtesy of R.B. Pickering.)

3. Skeletonized remains
4. Remains altered by extraordinary conditions such as fire, dismemberment, high impact trauma, or any one of many natural or induced methods.

In each scenario, the goal is to determine the identity of the person and to reconstruct the events surrounding his or her death. The less complete and more disturbed the remains, the more likely that a forensic anthropologist can and should be called to assist in recovery and examination. (Figure 1)

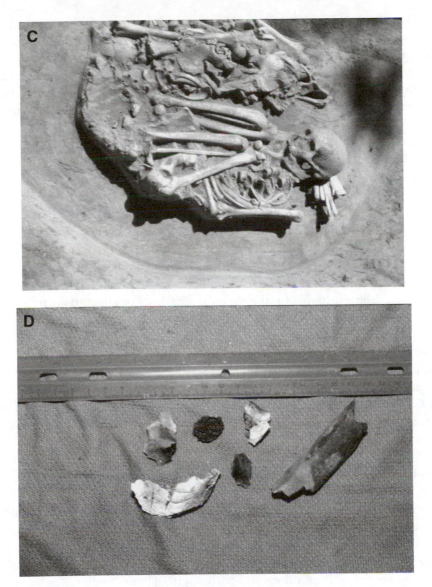

Figure 1 (continued)

Each of these scenarios can be divided into phases of activity. Traditionally, the forensic anthropologist was primarily involved with the last phase — examination. However, it is probable that the forensic anthropologist can aid in earlier phases such as the discovery and recovery phases. Discovery includes all of the work done up to the point at which the actual remains or gravesite is found. The recovery phase includes the work of removing the remains to the laboratory facility. In the lab, the formal examination or last phase begins.

The forensic goal, regardless of body condition or phase of investigatory activity, is to identify the remains and to determine the circumstances of the unexplained death. Ascertaining major biological characteristics such as age, sex, race/ethnicity, and stature are often the first pieces of data that help focus the investigation on specific group characteristics. Individual biological characteristics such as pattern of dental restoration, evidence of previous trauma and medical conditions, or unusual biological characteristics focus the search within a specific age/sex/race group. The forensic anthropologist can identify and determine these characteristics. Examining small structures on the skeleton and determining what they mean is the anthropologist's key contribution to forensic investigation. For example, small changes at joints such as the knee and elbow may indicate to the anthropologist that the person has suffered a particular type of injury in the past. A small bump on a bone may indicate the site of a well-healed fracture (Figure 2). An empty tooth socket might indicate either a tooth lost shortly before death or during the recovery. Evidence of healing separates the two. In summary, the forensic anthropologist can determine what on the skeleton is normal or abnormal, and which characteristics are of forensic significance and which ones are not.

Just as important as the biological characteristics of the remains is identifying the circumstances leading to the discovery of the remains and determining what has happened to the remains since death occurred. For example, determining whether or not the body was moved, time since death, and indications of trauma that might have occurred before, at the time of, or after death, are all critical elements that the forensic anthropologist often can provide in forensic cases.

When a remains is complete, determining sex, race/ethnicity, and stature can be done without great difficulty. The soft tissue provides the answers. In addition, tattoos, hair color and style, evidence of past surgery, or dental modifications provide individualizing characteristics that help identify remains. If the soft tissues and organs are intact, their analysis can reveal the kinds of information which may contribute to determination of the cause of, and events surrounding, death. Most often, the complete remains is examined by the medical examiner and pathologist. These cases are routine and the anthropologist is seldom involved.

However, the physical anthropologist may have a role to play on some occasions. An example comes from a rural county near an urban center where bodies of homicide victims often were dumped. The body of an adult, African-American male was recovered from the side of the road. The unusual circumstance of this case was that the head, hands, and feet had been severed from the body. Determining the "group characteristics" of sex and ethnicity was clear. Even determining the general age category was easy. Body size and body hair development clearly indicated that the person was a young adult.

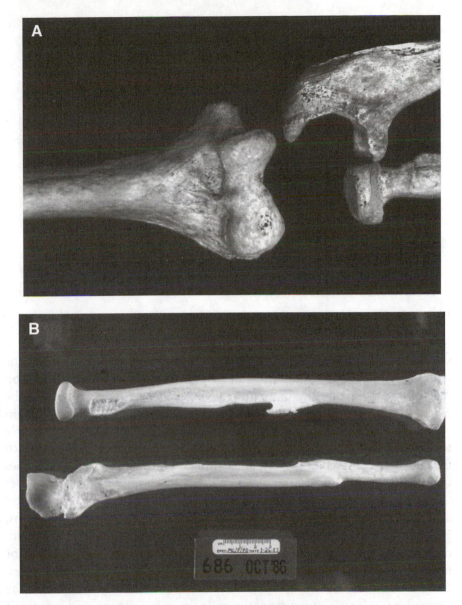

Figure 2 (A) An arthritic elbow joint shows change at the joint surfaces. (B) A healed fracture can be seen on the shafts of the radius and ulna. (Photos courtesy of R.B. Pickering.)

However, determining a more precise age range within the adult category required further examination. The severing destroyed the individualizing characteristics of the fingerprints and the head, perhaps the two most important portions in identifying intact remains. Without these portions, the anthropologist was asked to examine radiographs of the body to help refine

Figure 3 Detail of a corpse from which the hands, feet, and head had been severed. (Photo courtesy of R.B. Pickering.)

the age estimate and to look for potentially identifying characteristics on the bones that might be significant, or that might likely have been recorded on medical X-rays (Figure 3). The anthropologist was asked to help determine the height of the headless and footless corpse. In addition, a detailed examination by the anthropologist of the severed ends of the neck and limbs made it possible to determine the type of cutting instrument used and the direction from which the cuts were delivered. The traumatic cutting on the soft tissue and the bones themselves showed from which direction the body had been struck.

Decomposing remains present a more difficult situation for recovery and analysis. A medical examiner or pathologist should examine these remains. However, if the organs and other soft tissues are sufficiently deteriorated, determining the condition of the organs, identifying superficial trauma, or finding toxicological evidence may be impossible or nearly so. In such cases, a slightly different team of specialists should be consulted. In addition to the forensic pathologist, a forensic anthropologist, a radiologist, and a forensic entomologist all may contribute important insights.

Remains in the process of decomposing give off offensive odors and are difficult to handle, which nobody enjoys. For that reason, recovery and examination are difficult and may not be done in the detail they deserve. Yet, professional standards require that a systematic and complete examination must be conducted, because what seems apparent at first view may not hold true on closer inspection.

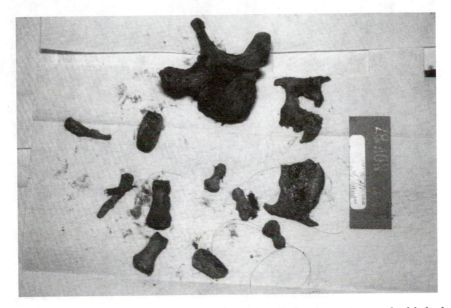

Figure 4   Remains found in a "second recovery" after investigators had left the scene. (Photo courtesy of R.B. Pickering.)

Take, for instance, two cases in which the remains displayed 50–75% soft tissue decomposition, yet at first inspection the skeletons appeared to be complete. On conducting a decidedly unpleasant yet necessary bone-by-bone inventory, it became clear that some elements of these remains were missing or had been altered. The decomposing tissue still adhering to the bones obscured important evidence. The inventory determined that the hyoid, a few phalanges, and at least one vertebra were missing. The missing hyoid could have been crucial evidence in both cases since homicide was a strong possibility. Because the recovery had been incomplete, a team including the anthropologist returned to the recovery site and within a few minutes the missing elements were recovered (Figure 4). In one case the hyoid was intact, but the ossified thyroid cartilage was fractured. (Figuare 5) This finding was important for two reasons. First, ossified thyroid cartilage, while not rare, is unusual. It is not part of the skeleton since it is ossified connective tissue not bone. Second, the cartilage was, in fact, fractured while the hyoid was not. This finding usually indicates compression of the throat and strangulation. However, because this and other elements were not found the first time, and because the site had been left unsecured for more than 24 hours, the significance of the fractured thyroid cartilage was questionable. There were conflicting indications as to whether or not the break was peri- or post-mortem. In addition, the investigators said that since the bones were found after the initial recovery, they did not think the evidence would be admissible in court.

Figure 5 A fractured ossified thyroid cartilage found after the initial recovery. Determining if the break was peri- or postmortem is crucial evidence. (Photo courtesy of R.B. Pickering.)

Fully skeletonized remains do not present soft tissue or organs that can be examined by pathologists. Forensic anthropologists are most likely to be called into this scenario. Forensic odontologists who specialize in identifying and analyzing the teeth and surrounding dental structures also may contribute expertise to this type of case. Much of the rest of this volume will discuss these kinds of cases.

In the scenario where remains are severely traumatized or otherwise altered, forensic anthropologists may also be valuable assets to the identification team. For more than three decades, forensic anthropologists have routinely helped in the recovery and analysis of civilian and military air crashes. In the early 1970s, forensic anthropologist Charles P. Warren, on staff at the U.S. Army CIL in Thailand, served a crucial role in the examination of a flight of orphans killed during the evacuation of Viet Nam. Two major factors affected the work in this case. First, the crash itself caused tremendous dismemberment, commingling, and destruction of body parts. Second, virtually all occupants were children of a similar age and ethnic affiliation. This sad case points to one more task often assumed by forensic anthropologists in mass disaster cases. In addition to identification and determination of cause of death, the need to separate commingled remains and to consolidate them into individuals is crucial.

Commingling of decomposing or skeletal remains creates one of the most difficult problems faced by an identification team. The goal in such cases is to determine how many persons are represented by the remains and then to consolidate the body parts into individuals. When fire and/or explosion severely traumatizes the remains, many details may be obscured. The situation represented by the planeload of young refugees had the additional problem of many individuals of about the same age killed and traumatically dismembered at the site. Commingling requires a team of specialists for recovery, identification, and data organization to make sure that no information is lost or misattributed.

As the investigator or medicolegal officer, you try to solve cases, determine causes of death, and identify remains. The preceding discussion should make it clear that a forensic anthropologist can make valuable contributions in each of the four scenarios identified at the beginning of this section. Finding a forensic anthropologist and developing a good working relationship can be helpful. Once you have decided to work with a forensic anthropologist, finding a person with academic training and field experience is crucial. Forensic anthropology is an unusual specialty that requires much training and experience. As the medicolegal officer, you need to be certain that you have the right people on your team. Taking a few courses in physical anthropology or watching the recovery of a body is insufficient training to call yourself a forensic anthropologist.

How to Find a Forensic Anthropologist

Within the forensic field, there is one principal organization to which forensic anthropologists are likely to belong — the American Academy of Forensic Sciences, Anthropology Section. In addition, a person may belong to regional or international forensic organizations and may be a Diplomate of the American Board for Forensic Anthropology, Inc. Your interview process could be shortened by asking about these credentials, first. However, not every jurisdiction has a forensic anthropologist who is a member of these organizations. Therefore, it is still important for the investigator to determine the level of training and experience held by any potential anthropological consultant.

Determining if there is a bona fide forensic anthropologist in your jurisdiction can be accomplished by calling the office of the American Academy of Forensic Sciences at (719) 636-1100 in Colorado Springs, CO, and asking about the location of members in your state or region. At the end of 1995, there were 75 Fellows and active Members of the Anthropology Section, but

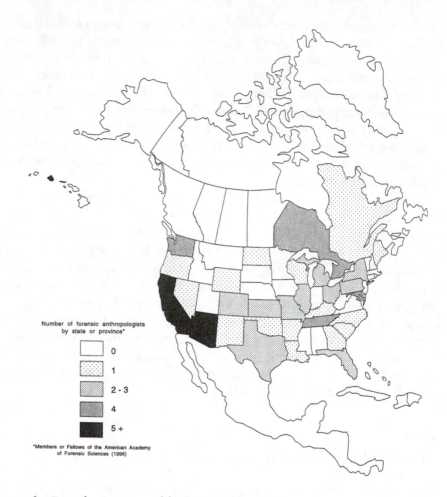

Number of forensic anthropologists
by state or province*

☐ 0
1
2 - 3
4
5 +

*Members or Fellows of the American Academy
of Forensic Sciences (1996)

Figure 6   Distribution map of forensic anthropologists who are members of the
American Academy of Forensic Sciences in 1996.

they are not evenly distributed over the country: they are concentrated at the
U.S. Army CIL in Hawaii, at the University of Tennessee, and in Washington,
D.C. Only Kentucky has a state forensic anthropologist, and in some states
there are no forensic anthropologists at all (Figure 6).

In order to reap the maximum benefit from working with a forensic
anthropologist, there are some basic questions that you should ask a potential
consultant. The answers you receive can help you select a well-qualified
forensic anthropologist.

In some sense, the questions are the same kind that you would ask any
potential expert regarding their scientific education and training. However,
because of the specialized nature of forensic anthropology, actual case experience
is a primary consideration. In terms of education, it is virtually impossible to

get the training needed in a four-year bachelor's program at any university. A master's degree in anthropology is the minimum that one should expect. A master's specialization in forensic anthropology would be ideal and can be obtained at the University of Tennessee. At this writing, the principal professors in the University of Arizona and University of New Mexico forensic anthropology programs have retired, and the future of these programs is in doubt. Beyond the master's level, there are ABDs (all but dissertation) and Ph.D's. At both of these levels, the individual specializes in some aspect of human anatomy or osteology, bioanthropology, or paleopathology. It is important to remember that not all physical anthropologists work with humans and not all human-oriented anthropologists work with bones. People in other anthropological specialties, such as archaeology and even cultural anthropology may be helpful on some topics such as how to excavate a site, how to differentiate animal from human bones, or how to identify clothing or jewelry from another country. As helpful as they are, these specialists will not be able to provide the detailed skeletal observations that you need, the kind that can be done by a forensic anthropologist.

As part of the interview process, you should determine the variety and levels of training and experience the candidate has had. For example, has the person participated in any archaeological excavations to learn proper recovery and recording techniques? Archaeological field schools are the best place to gain experience and learn proper excavation and data recording techniques. Has the person participated in one or more field schools? Your candidate should have participated in at least one field school for one season; however, that is an absolute minimum. Did they supervise an excavation? As in most fields, supervising others helps one learn the job. Supervising an excavation adds the organizational and management skills that are valuable on a forensic team. Does their experience include directing a laboratory? It is in the laboratory that remains are cleaned, data and samples are organized and documented, and detailed examinations are conducted. Laboratory experience on a field project is an important element of training. Has the person ever written a report on their research? A list of publications and/or a sample of their forensic publications will help you evaluate the candidate's work.

For direct osteological experience, one of the best questions to ask is how many skeletons has the person examined and in what context? Forensic anthropology, like virtually all other forensic specialties, is an applied science. The more skeletal cases examined, the wider the anthropologist's range of experience. Physical anthropologists who work with archaeologically recovered material may have examined hundreds or even thousands of human skeletal remains (Figure 7). They may have seen a wide range of ages of skeletons and degrees of preservation. However, it also may be likely that they have seen skeletons mainly from one small geographic region. Anthropologists

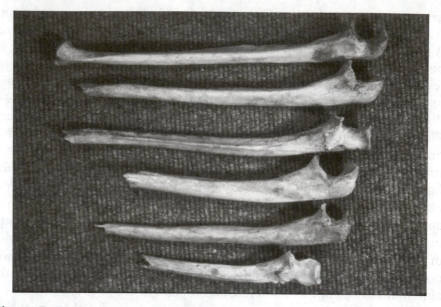

Figure 7 Archaeological sites sometimes yield large numbers of skeletons or portions of human remains. These ulnae were part of an ossuary in which a large number of commingled remains were found. (Photo courtesy of R.B. Pickering.)

who were trained primarily on cadaver or museum collections also may have worked with a large number of skeletons, sometimes from many parts of the world. However, they may not have had direct experience in recovering human remains from the ground.

The point is that people come into forensic anthropology from a number of different directions. As the medicolegal officer, you need to ascertain the kind and level of experience of the potential consultant. It would be entirely appropriate to ask the potential forensic anthropologist for references, just as you would in a job interview. In fact, you are conducting a job interview.

Establishing the Ground Rules

Once you have found a forensic anthropologist and determined that this person's qualifications fit your needs, additional discussion should be started to outline your working relationship. You need to tell the forensic anthropologist what you expect of them and they need to tell you what they expect of your office. That discussion should include everything from who provides various kinds of equipment, who takes and who may use photographs, fee structure, acceptable response time both at the site and for timely delivery of the report, and general format of reports. Other subjects also may arise, but these are some of the basic points upon which understanding should be reached in advance.

There are no hard and fast rules concerning these aspects of work; however, there are some accepted practices that might be helpful to review. The timing for sharing information is important regardless of the other aspects of the case. For example, forensic anthropologists do not like to know, in advance, the particulars of the person's remains they are examining — even if you are nearly certain that you know the identity of the deceased. Giving the anthropologist details about what should be found may bias their results. Anthropologists do, however, want to know about the context of the case if they have not participated in the recovery. Any photos, drawings, videotapes, or other media that were used to record the discovery and recovery should be made available to them. Access to the actual personal effects or pictures of them also should be made available.

The following fictitious conversation, which takes place at the beginning of a recovery of a skeleton, is an example of giving information to the anthropologist before it is needed.

> "Well, Doc, we found this skeleton in a well behind the old Smith place. The old man has been missing for about three years. Just disappeared. He was just a month short of his sixtieth, too. Sort of a short, scrawny guy, no more than 5'7". Skinny, too. By the way, he broke his leg in a farm accident about five years before he died. I talked to the town dentist. He said that if there was a full set of upper and lower dentures, it was ol' man Smith."

While the investigator thinks he is being helpful by offering all these details, in fact, he is creating a problem for the anthropologist. The anthropologist needs to establish the biological profile of the deceased independently, without preconceptions of what results should be found. Independence allows the anthropologist to work without bias. Equally important, when the anthropologist works independently, the investigator can have more confidence in the accuracy of the findings. Should this kind of case come to court, the independence and lack of bias could be important issues.

As stated previously, anthropologists need to know about the context of the case, in advance. Details of the type of ground cover, whether the remains is partially or completely skeletal, and whether it is on the ground surface or buried help the anthropologist prepare for the recovery and analysis. Only the purported identity and biological characteristics of the deceased should not be discussed in advance of recovery.

Now let's take a more detailed look at the ground rules for working effectively with your forensic anthropologist. In order to make the most efficient use of everyone's time, the investigator should discuss in advance which supplies and services will be provided by which person or office. For example, you should expect that a forensic anthropologist will provide excavation and recovery tools such as trowels, brushes, notebooks, tape recorder, etc. The following is a list of basic equipment needed at the recovery site by the forensic anthropologist. This list should be considered as the absolute minimum of equipment. Additional digging and screening equipment is usually a good idea. Similarly, recording the data verbally and as images is critical. Therefore, using video equipment, tape recorders, etc., is recommended.

- Short-handled sharpened shovel
- Trowel
- Screen (@18" sq.) — ⅛" mesh
- Screen (@24" sq.) — ¼" mesh
- Bamboo picks
- Dental picks
- Graph paper for mapping
- Plumb bob
- Line levels
- String
- Flagging pins
- Compass
- Directional arrow marked off in inches or centimeters
- Two tape measures (20' or 50' lengths)
- 2 carpenter's rules
- Pencils and pens with indelible ink
- Paper and plastic bags of different sizes for specimens
- Paper labels for specimen bags
- Film canisters or small jars for small specimens
- 35-mm camera (2 cameras, one with color slide film and the second with black and white print film are preferred)
- Additional close-up lens
- Flash attachment
- Color and black and white film

At recovery sites such as plane crashes or explosions where special or protective gear is needed, the anthropologist will depend on you to provide it. The anthropologist will expect the law enforcement office or coroner to provide site security, people to record and recover non-skeletal evidence, and someone to talk to the news media.

Photographs are an important part of any case file; they are also important for the forensic anthropologist who will use them to record important details of the remains. For example, most anthropologists photograph characteristics on the skeleton that are used in determining age, sex, or other biological characteristics such as trauma, dental restoration, or other unusual characteristics. These photos provide a long-term record to help the anthropologist remember exactly what the remains revealed. That information is of obvious importance should the forensic anthropologist have to testify in court. In addition, most forensic anthropologists conduct research on forensic topics. Case photos may be used in future research projects. Allowing the forensic anthropologist to take and keep photos is standard practice. Not allowing the forensic anthropologist to photograph remains unnecessarily limits the educational potential of casework. If your office has a staff photographer, that person and the forensic anthropologist should decide who will be responsible for recording specific kinds of data. For example, the staff photographer may do all of the recovery scene shots, evidentiary materials, and general pictures of the remains while the forensic anthropologist photographs details pertinent to the remains themselves.

In addition to photos, the forensic anthropologist may request to cast parts of the remains or to take occasional samples. For example, it may be appropriate to take casts of the dentition or the pubic symphyses. Casts create a tangible record which has value in court, in research, and in the classroom. If taking casts is allowed, a letter of agreement (see sidebar) defining how they may be used is appropriate. For example, having actual casts from known-age and known-sex individuals is useful for teaching future generations of anthropologists and investigators. Taking actual samples of bone may be requested so that additional testing can be conducted. For example, if determining age is not possible by normal visual examination, taking a small section of bone for osteon counting might be requested. Bone samples also might be required for determining the ABO blood group, DNA, or presence of heavy metals or drugs. Permission to keep physical remains must be compatible with all appropriate laws and practices and should be documented in a letter of agreement that ideally is signed prior to the beginning of an investigation.

The fee structure for anthropological services varies by region and individual. However, remember that a forensic anthropologist is a highly trained specialist with many years of academic training. Medical doctors and lawyers are not expected to work for free. You do not expect to work for free and neither should you expect the forensic anthropologist to give his services for free. As usual though, there are exceptions to the rule. For example, many anthropologists, when asked to look at a bone to determine whether or not it is human, do not charge. In most cases they can quickly say that it is or is not human. Because one of the authors, Robert Pickering, works at the

Letters of Agreement

Printed here are examples of letters of agreement that you might use as models for letters between your office and consulting forensic anthropologists. However, they are only models. Actual wording should be discussed in advance with the anthropologist and the final letter should be reviewed by your office's legal advisor.

Dear Forensic Anthropologist:

This letter constitutes my permission for you to use photographs of forensic cases on which you consulted for my office. Photos may be used for teaching purposes and as references to past cases. Photos also may be used in professional articles or books. However, the following stipulations apply:

1. The name of the deceased cannot be used or published without prior written consent of this office.

2. No photos can be published without prior written consent of this office. You should provide one copy of the publication in a timely manner to this office.

3. If the photo was taken by a staff photographer, a credit line should appear with the photo. For example, "Photo provided by the Alpha County Coroner's Office."

4. This permission does not apply to use of case photos by other persons and cannot be transferred by you to another person.

5. Any use of photos from cases in this jurisdiction, beyond training of students and colleagues, which is not specified in this letter, must be approved in writing by this office.

By signing this letter and returning it to me, you signify your agreement with and willingness to abide by the terms of the letter.

Respectfully,

_____   _____

Alpha County Coroner   Forensic Anthropologist

Date: Date:

Dear Forensic Anthropologist:

   This letter constitutes my permission for you to make casts of skeletal specimens from forensic cases on which you consulted for my office. Casts may be used for teaching purposes and as references to past cases. However, the following stipulations apply:

1. The process of creating a cast cannot damage or alter any portion of the bone.

2. You must provide to me in writing a protocol for how the casts are made. Include a list of all chemicals or materials that will come in contact with the bone and a description of the casting process, including times for each portion of the process.

3. You must specify the number of casts made and be able to account for them at all times. Each cast should be labeled with the case number of this office.

4. Casts may not be given away, traded, sold, or otherwise dispersed to other individuals.

5. If casts are no longer serviceable or if you no longer need them for instructional purposes, all casts should be returned to this office.

   By signing this letter and returning it to me, you signify your agreement with and willingness to abide by the terms of the letter.

Respectfully,

_____   _____

Alpha County Coroner   Forensic Anthropologist

Date: Date:

Denver Museum of Natural History, he can go a step further. He compares the bone to skeletons in the Zoology Department's osteology collections in order to determine the genus or species of the animal from which the bone came (Figure 8). While this extra step is not absolutely necessary, it gives Pickering and the investigator greater confidence in the identification.

Figure 8   All three bones are metatarsal bones of deer. The one in the middle is weathered and the others are study specimens. (Photo courtesy of Rick Wicker/DMNH.)

If the bone specimen is identified as human, a search and recovery operation may be required. Usually anthropologists charge an hourly rate for fieldwork and laboratory examination, plus expenses. If the case is large and complex, establishing a weekly or monthly rate may be more appropriate. Fees can scare medicolegal officers, particularly those from rural or otherwise lightly inhabited jurisdictions. As they begin to mentally calculate the potential cost, a picture of an entire year's budget disappearing on one case may come to mind. While that is a possibility, it is virtually unheard of for a forensic anthropologist to refuse to work on a case because of insufficient remuneration. They are professionals and they serve. The terms professional and service are both important.

The Case Report

The purpose of an anthropologist's report should be stated clearly. The case report records physical observations on the remains, identifies important biological characteristics, identifies and differentiates changes in the remains due to natural and cultural forces, and *provides this information in a meaningful and understandable form to the medicolegal officer in charge.* As part of the preliminary understanding between you and the forensic anthropologist, a report format should be agreed upon. Examples are given at the end of this chapter.

The report is generated by the anthropologist after careful examination, research, and reflection. To a large extent, the complexity of the case will determine how long this process takes. The anthropologist's report should provide the most detailed and precise data that can be provided at the time. However, that does not mean the report cannot be modified. If a statement is unclear, or if the clues that lead to a particular conclusion do not make sense to you, it is reasonable for you to ask for further clarification. If additional technical tests are conducted, that information should be given to the anthropologist for consideration. Any new evidence may require a new look at the anthropologist's findings.

A caution concerning reports; they need to be written, *not verbal*. It is always a bad idea to press the anthropologist for detailed and positive determinations during the recovery phase or the initial parts of the examination phase. Speculation is dangerous for you and the anthropologist. While any investigator, including anthropologists, makes observations and may be mulling over various ideas while in the field, these are not final results and may change once all the data has been reviewed. Although everyone wants the results as soon as possible, rushing to conclusions doesn't save time; instead it costs time, effort, and credibility.

The anthropologist's report should provide a succinct determination of results which can be substantiated by the data. In general, each major biological characteristic should be identified. The anthropologist should state conclusions as clearly and unequivocally as possible. The advice of the former commander of the U.S. Army CIL, Lt. Colonel Harold Tucker, relates: "If you are going to sign your name to a report, say what you need to say clearly. If you cannot support it, don't say it!" However, if a conclusion is tentative, it should be stated in that manner and accepted as such.

At times, the medicolegal officer may ask the forensic anthropologist to address specific points of information such as identifying the probable cause of trauma on a remains or determination of time since death. The report should include a discussion of how each result was reached. However, a full discussion of techniques and the reasoning behind the use of one technique over another may not be helpful; rather, it may confuse and get in the way of the actual results. Additionally, the most useful reports are complete, yet concise. The report should avoid conclusions that cannot be substantiated within the anthropologist's sphere of knowledge. Anthropologists do not know everything, and their written comments should be limited to their expertise. You may damage your case anytime you ask for or accept statements from people who are willing to speak on subjects beyond their fields.

Case Report Samples

The following examples of reports are presented to clarify the kind of information best supplied by the forensic anthropologist. The format was developed by the author, Robert Pickering, from over 15 years of consultation. His format works, but so do others. The first page of the report is a listing of the major biological characteristics and other observations such as timing of trauma observed on the remains. The information in each category is purposefully brief and clear. The second part of the format provides a more detailed explanation of how each variable was determined.

This report format provides accurate and pertinent information in a manner that is understandable and useful to medical and police investigators. The first page, with its brief biological profile, can be used to start a missing person search and can be released to a wide circle of people who might need to know some of the general aspects of the case. The second part of the form, with its explanations, is useful for the investigators and pathologists who may need more detail. Experience has shown that one format does not serve the purposes of all people involved in death investigations. The format presented here attempts to resolve that problem.

These examples present different kinds of cases. The first is a complete adult skeleton. The forensic anthropologist was brought into the case when the skeleton was already at the Medical Examiner's office. The second case was a body drastically altered by fire. The forensic anthropologist was called to the site and conducted the recovery with the assistance of coroner's and sheriff's personnel. The third case involved a nearly complete remains. Again, the anthropologist saw it in the lab and did not take part in the recovery. Soft tissue and most organs were generally intact. As you review these examples you will note that although many of the basic procedures of examination did not change, the condition of the remains and amount of data are different. These examples clearly show that the number of characteristics which can be determined does vary with the completeness of the remains.

Summary of Physical Characteristics
Case XXX — Sept. 1986

Sex:	Male
Age:	55–70 Years
Race:	Caucasoid
Height:	5'5"–5'7"
Handedness:	Right
Ante-mortem Trauma:	Numerous facial fractures; 3 ribs (left); 2 ribs (right); 1st metacarpal (right)

Peri-mortem Trauma: Extensive fracture across the face and extending to the left temporal

Pathology: Extensive degenerative joint disease; ante-mortem tooth loss; caries; periostitis at left ankle

Build: Short and robust

Explanation of Physical Characteristics
Case XXX — Sept. 1986

Sex — All pertinent morphological characteristics of the pelvis and skull indicate that the remains are male. Characteristics on the pelvis include a narrow sciatic notch, narrow subpubic angle, and the alae are high and relatively narrow. Cranial characteristics include a very prominent supraorbital ridge, large mastoid process, and robust nuchal crest. There are no morphological characteristics which would indicate the female sex.

Age — All of the epiphyses of long bones and the basi-occipital suture are fused. Therefore, the individual is definitely an adult. All of the major endocranial sutures are closed, thus indicating an age of 45+ years. Morphological features of the pubic symphyses also indicate advanced age, at least 55+ years of age. Lack of accepted morphological features make it very difficult to assign an upper age limit to people in the older adult category. The best estimate, however, is 55–70 years of age.

Race — Characteristics of the facial portion of the skull were used to determine race. In general the skull has a long narrow shape. It lacks prognathism and robust malar elements. It should be noted, however, that both zygomatics present healed fractures. The nasal elements are particularly important. The nasals are thin throughout their length and are ridged. The nasal aperture is relatively long and narrow and presents a sharp nasal sill. All of these features are compatible with Caucasoid features and are not compatible with negroid or mongoloid features.

Height — Determining an accurate height estimate was difficult because of destruction of the ends of long bones by rodents. In almost all cases, the superior and inferior articular surfaces were totally eaten away. Only the right fibula was complete enough to get a precise measurement on its total length. Although, the humeri were damaged, they were complete enough to provide a usable estimate of their length. In addition, Steele's formula for reconstructing the length of long bones from their specified segments was used to estimate the length of the tibia. That estimated length was then used to estimate stature of the individual. The following figures show that all of the elements provided similar estimates.

A. Right fibula (36.1 cm)
    Height estimate   66.1" ——— **67.4"** ——— 68.73"
B. Left humerus (32.3 cm),
       right humerus (32.2 cm)
    Height estimate   66.23" ——— **67.9"** ——— 69.47"
C. Right tibia (est. 35.9 cm)
    Height estimate   66.29" ——— **67.64"** ——— 68.98"

In this case, three height estimates were calculated on three different bones. For each bone, the low and high end of the range as well as the central height estimate are provided. Note that all three estimates are similar but not identical. The anthropologist uses all of these measurements to refine the final height estimate.

Because of the person's age, it is appropriate to reduce the stature estimate. While regression formulas result in the estimates listed above, approximately one inch should be subtracted from those figures. I suggest the best estimate as being 65"-67".

Handedness — From the size of the glenoid fossa on the scapula, morphology of the scapula and size of the humeri, it is probable that the individual was right handed.

Ante-mortem trauma — There is evidence of numerous healed fractures on the facial portion of the skull. Both nasal bones and adjacent portions of the maxillae have been broken and healed. The nasals are deviated to the left. Both zygomatic bones have been broken and healed. In both cases, the fractures were at or near the zygotemporal symphysis. There is a noticeable thinning in these areas and a slight displacement at this junction of the zygomatics and temporals.

Three ribs on the left side of the body have been broken and are now healed. Left ribs 10, 11, and 12 appear to have healed without serious complication. On the right side, ribs 9 and 10 also indicate healed fractures.

The right first metacarpal has been badly damaged by rodent gnawing. However, it is obvious that the bone has been fractured near its proximal end and later healed. The fracture appears to have been complicated by possible infection. There is hyperostosis and ankylosis with an adjacent carpal element.

Peri-mortem trauma — There is a major unhealed trauma which diagonally crosses the face of the skull and the left temporal bone. A small portion of bone along the nasal sill of the right maxilla has been fractured away. The contiguous portion of the left maxilla is bent rather than completely fractured. A fracture line is visible running from the nasal margin of the left maxilla and extends diagonally down to the area above the upper molars on the left side. Another fracture line extends from the nasal margin of the right maxilla to the maxillozygomatic symphysis. The fracture then bifurcates: one side extending up to the lower portion of the right orbit, and the second branch extending down along the symphysis line between the maxilla and zygoma. A fracture line also crosses the base of the left sphenoid, extends across, and bisects the left temporal.

There is no evidence of healing on any of these fractures. There is no discoloration which might indicate that they are recent, i.e., they do not appear to be the result of improper recovery or care. The fracture pattern would indicate that all of these fractures could have resulted from the same traumatic event.

Pathology — The dentition shows poor dental health. There is only one cavity, although it is a large one. Most of the dentin has been destroyed and only the hollow enamel shell of the upper right canine remains. There is a probable abscess at the alveolus of the upper right first molar. At least 10 teeth have been lost before death. Their sockets are in various stages of resorption. The remaining teeth show calculus deposits along the gumline. Another 10 teeth have been lost after death. There is no resorption at their sockets.

On virtually all long bone joints that are observable, there is evidence of degenerative joint disease. Vertebrae also present considerable degenerative change. The second and third cervical vertebrae show partial ankylosis on the left side. The lower cervicals and upper thoracics all have marked lipping on the body of the vertebrae. The sixth thoracic vertebra is wedged as a result of compression stress and degeneration. There is a probable Schmorl's nodule affecting the tenth and eleventh thoracic vertebrae.

There is initial ligament ossification on the superior surfaces of the sacrum and adjacent areas of the ilia, just above the sacroiliac junction. There is no ankylosis. However, the ossification would be visible on radiographs of the area.

There is degeneration and periostitis on the distal portion of the left fibula. Examination of the adjacent tarsals revealed evidence of some initial ligament ossification and erosion of the articular surface between calcaneus and cuboid. It is probable that the extent of this degeneration would cause some disability, possibly a limp.

Build — Although the long bones are relatively short, they have rugged areas of muscle attachment. The humeri and ulnae are particularly rugous.

Summary — A generalized description of the remains would include the following characteristics. The individual was a short, stocky white male in his late 50s or 60s. He led a life that was physically stressful as indicated by muscularity and degenerative change. Numerous examples of healed trauma also may indicate a physically stressful life. Trauma to the face might have resulted in some disfigurement. Certainly, the formerly broken nose would be obvious. The man may have walked with a limp which favored the left leg. The thumb of the right hand probably did not have a full range of motion.

Summary of Physical Characteristics
Case YYY — 1994

Age:	Adult.
Sex:	Male?
Race:	Indeterminate.
Height:	Indeterminate.
Stature:	Indeterminate.
Handedness:	Indeterminate.
Distinguishing dental traits:	The left lower lateral incisor was lost ante-mortem and the socket has totally resorbed. A three-tooth ceramic bridge was found in the area of the head. It appears to correspond with the lost incisor.
Pathology:	None observed.
Ante-mortem trauma:	None observed.
Peri-mortem trauma:	None observed.
Post-mortem trauma:	Extreme discoloration, fragmentation, and destruction of bone because of exposure to intense long-term burning.
Post-mortem disturbance:	Some scattering of the bones occurred during and after incineration. An additional thin (1–3 in.) layer of dirt was then thrown on the remains. A second smaller burning episode occurred on top of the dirt layer.
Disposition of the body:	The body was laying on the left side with arms and legs flexed; a wristwatch band and metal studs from clothing were found among the bones indicating that they were with the body at the time of incineration.
Time since death:	Less than 2 years.

Explanation of Physical Characteristics
Case YYY — 1994

Age — Adult. All epiphyses of long bones that were present are fused. The third molar was erupted and the root tip was closed.

Sex — Male? The size and robusticity of the long bones suggests that the individual was male.

Race — Indeterminate. No diagnostic criteria.

Height — Indeterminate. Long bones were too fragmentary to be used as a basis for height estimation.

Stature — Indeterminate. Remains were too incomplete to determine this trait.

Handedness — Indeterminate. No comparable left and right arm elements are measurable.

Distinguishing dental traits — The left lower lateral incisor was lost ante-mortem and the socket has totally resorbed. A three-tooth ceramic bridge was found in the area of the head. It appears to correspond with the lost incisor. A forensic odontologist should examine these remains.

Pathology — None observed.

Ante-mortem trauma — None observed.

Peri-mortem trauma — None observed.

Post-mortem trauma — Extreme discoloration, fragmentation, and destruction of bone because of exposure to intense long-term burning. Much of the bone is calcined, that is burned gray to white, cracked, and warped.

Post-mortem disturbance — Some scattering of the bones occurred during and after incineration as evidenced by finding bone fragments in different parts of the burning area. An additional thin (1–3 in.) layer of dirt was then thrown on the remains after the fire had subsided. No discoloration of the dirt on top was evident. Thus it had been deposited after the fire cooled. A second smaller burning episode occurred on top of the dirt layer. It was not an intense fire in that it did not discolor the underlying layer.

Disposition of the body — The body was laying on the left side with arms and legs flexed. The head lay toward the northeast and the feet to the southwest. Bones of the forearms and hands, and the wristwatch band were found together and indicate that the bones were in anatomical position. The two forearms were together or slightly crossed. They were positioned in front of the upper chest. The back was adjacent to the left side of the interior of the fire pit as evidenced by the vertebral elements recovered. Bones of the leg and feet found on the right side of the fire pit. A wristwatch band and metal studs from clothing were found among the bones indicating that they were with the body at the time of incineration.

Time since death — Less than 2 years. Moisture in the bone layer was frozen and there was snow on top of the bone layer. Ash from the second (most recent) fire was adhering to the underside of the snow. Much of the bone was exposed directly under the snow. The dirt layer between the two burning episodes was soft. Under the bone an ash layer was evidence of previous fires. The twig and bark residues were different in texture, content, and compactness from the ash and charcoal residue in the incineration layer.

Summary of Physical Characteristics
Case ZZZ — 1992

Age:	20–24 years.
Sex:	Male.
Race:	Caucasian?
Tattoos:	Tattoos were visible on both sides of the thorax.
Pathology:	Many episodes of dental intervention.
Ante-mortem trauma:	Healed fracture of right nasal bone.
Peri-mortem trauma:	Two blunt instrument strikes to right supraorbital ridge and related fracture to right orbital roof; incomplete fracture of right wing of hyoid, fractured enamel of right upper canine tooth.
Post-mortem trauma:	None.
Post-mortem disturbance:	No animal, insect, or mechanical disturbance.

Explanation of Physical Characteristics
Case ZZZ — 1992

Identification — Ante-mortem dental records and radiographs for John Doe were compared with the dentition and post-mortem dental radiographs. The records were compatible. There were no unexplainable incompatibilities. Other major physical characteristics were compatible with this identity. There were no incompatible characteristics.

Age — 20–24 years. The medial clavicles are fusing. The basi-occipital suture was fused. Examination of the pubic symphyses indicates the age range of 20–24 years.

Sex — Male. The remains was complete enough for a visual examination of external genitalia and determination of sex as male.

Race — Caucasian? The face is relatively long and narrow. Face is not broad. The nasal aperture has a sharp lower rim and is relatively high and broad. The nasal bones are ridged at their common suture and are narrow.

Tattoos — A tattoo was visible on each side of the chest. The anthropologist did not examine them in detail.

Pathology — Many episodes of dental intervention. The dentition evidences one well-healed extraction and one that was in the process of healing at time of death. There are many filings and one probable pulp extraction at the lower left first molar. All fillings appear to be amalgam except the filling on the upper left first incisor which is a material that approximates the color of enamel. See attached dental chart.

Antemortem trauma — Healed fracture of right nasal bone. The right anterior portion of the nasal bone was fractured but has healed.

Perimortem trauma — Two blunt instrument strikes to right supraorbital ridge and related fracture to right orbital roof. One strike was to medial portion of the supraorbital ridge. There is a fracture approximately 10 mm in length that runs superior and perpendicular from the medial ridge. The second strike impacted the frontozygomatic suture. Both strikes resulted in a detachment of a piece of bone. Viewed from inside the cranium, a fracture to the right orbital roof is clearly visible. It is related to the strike to the supraorbital. There is an incomplete fracture of the right wing of the hyoid. Morphology of the hyoid fracture indicates that pressure was applied from lateral to medial. The occlusal portion of the right upper canine tooth enamel has been fractured away.

Postmortem trauma — None.

Postmortem disturbance — No animal, insect, or mechanical disturbance. The remains was recovered in a heavy plastic bag which had been buried.

Techniques for Recovering Skeletonized Human Remains

4

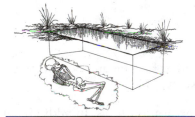

Although every forensic case is different, each case goes through many of the same phases. Each phase requires its own procedures and expertise. Throughout each phase, the chain of evidence must remain intact. The first phase usually is the discovery of the case. As likely as not, discovery is made by the public. The second phase is recovery of the remains and evidence. This and future phases require professional help. Next, laboratory analysis of remains and evidence and research into the case proceeds. At some point, all of the data from the different labs and investigators come together and are synthesized into the case report. Although changes may be made, this synthesis is the formal interpretation of the data and provides the most logical explanation or reconstruction of the events.

Proper and complete recovery of human remains is critical to the resolution of the case. The reverse of that statement is also true. If the recovery is incomplete or poorly executed, major problems are likely to be encountered in solving the case. As discussed in the third chapter, finding the right forensic anthropologist and being prepared in advance can help assure efficient resolution of a case. Just as important, planning strategy and organizing equipment in advance can facilitate recovery.

Equipment Requirements

From the anthropologist's viewpoint, the basic equipment list for field recovery includes tools of excavation: shovels, trowels, screens, various measuring instruments, storage, and labeling material. Your office should always have a

Figure 9   A portable screen is invaluable in finding remains and evidence at the recovery site. (Drawing courtesy of L. Schulzkump, M.D.)

few shovels available as well as other hand excavation tools. In addition, at least two screens should be available: ¼- and ⅛-in. mesh hardware screens are basic. For the ¼-in. mesh, the screen which is 18–24 in. on a side can be used effectively. For the ⅛-in. mesh, a 12–18 in. screen is convenient. Figure 9 is an example of a ¼-in. screen. Depending on the kind of case, even finer mesh screens may be useful. As discussed in Chapter 3, it is essential that the forensic anthropologist and the investigator in charge of the case agree what equipment and personnel each will provide before beginning a recovery.

The investigator in charge needs to think about equipment and personnel in a broader context. At a minimum, the equipment list should include material to secure the site, to provide communication with all necessary law enforcement and medical agencies, and to document evidence. Personnel to handle all of these functions also is required. In addition, a person designated to handle news media can help provide information without impeding the work. The most important person is the one in charge and able to make decisions. This person directs the work flow and assures that everyone knows their task and works efficiently.

Recovery activities might be broken down into three categories. In the first, someone has said they think they know where a remains can be found. If the statement is credible, your job is to find those remains. In the second category, someone brings a bone or bones to you. Your first step is to find out if the bone is human. If it is, you have a skeleton to find. In the final case, you are presented with the entire set of bones. Although well meaning, the person has given you a difficult job since none of the remains are now in their original context. Your job is to try to reconstruct that context.

Each of these recovery scenarios requires a slightly different approach. However, some characteristics are common to each. All the above-mentioned scenarios include skeletonized human remains. In the following section, each scenario will be discussed and explained with examples from past cases.

"I Think There's a Skeleton Buried in This Field"

In some cases, finding remains is a difficult task. Therefore, discovery of the remains precedes recovery. Sometimes, the region of probable disposal is known fairly precisely and sometimes it is not. Depending on the precision of location, different techniques will be needed. Obviously, the investigator will try to obtain specific information from informants regarding the location of a body. The more information provided, the more efficient the search. However, time passes, seasons change, and the informant may not be able to pinpoint the location precisely. In such a case, the environment itself may provide clues to the previous disposal of a body. Forensic anthropologists, particularly those with archaeological training, can help with the discovery process. They are experienced in observing natural and artificial changes in soils, plants, and insect communities. A truism of archaeology is that anything done to the soil leaves a record.

Archaeologists routinely "read" the soil to determine what kinds of natural and cultural changes have occurred. Throughout the U.S., as well as in other countries, it is not uncommon to find pits, trenches, or other earth-moving activities that can be dated at hundreds or even thousands of years of age. By removing dirt, the natural stratigraphy and the compact nature of the soil is disturbed. Even if the same soil is put back in the pit, it will not have the same compactness, color pattern, and structure as the undisturbed soil. Great age does not mean that soil disturbances have been obliterated. The forensic time scale of a few weeks or decades, rather than hundreds or thousands of years, means that many changes in the soil that might indicate a clandestine interment are still visible to the knowledgeable eye.

Figure 10 shows a round break in the plastered floor of a building that is over 1200 years old. Simply removing the dirt above the floor and sweeping the surface revealed a pit that held ancient human remains. A much more recent example, Figure 11 is the intentional interment of a Japanese soldier on the Island of Yap. The grave dates from the last year of World War II. The dark soil is the fill in the grave pit and is distinct from the surrounding natural soil. A characteristic of soil on Yap is that it is acidic and has a high moisture content. Even though the pit shape has been well preserved, excavation of the grave revealed that the bones had virtually disintegrated. After no more than 35 years in the ground only a few enamel tooth crowns and remnants of eyeglasses and boot soles remained (Figure 12). The paradox here is that while the soil clearly revealed the location of the remains, soil conditions destroyed most of the skeletal evidence.

Similar to these two early examples, pits containing more recently interred bodies can be discovered from a detailed examination of the ground surface. In addition to the clues provided by the soil texture, color, and

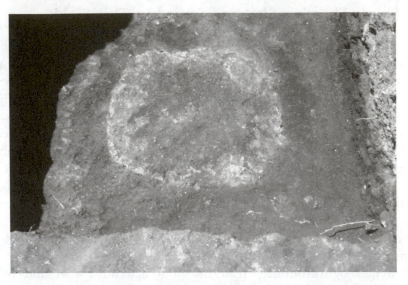

Figure 10 With the right soil conditions and proper excavation, pits which are older than 1500 years can easily be revealed. (Photo courtesy of R.B. Pickering.)

Figure 11 Although this pit dates near the end of World War II, virtually no skeletal remains were recovered because of poor preservation. (Photo courtesy of R.B. Pickering.)

compactness, the vegetation on and around the pit may be useful. In virtually all parts of the country there are a succession of plants that begin to grow anytime the soil has been disturbed. The name often given to the first arrivals on disturbed soil is "volunteer plant" (Figure 13). Contacting a local botanist

Figure 12   Personal effects recovered from a Japanese grave dated 1944. Only a few tooth crowns survived because of the high soil acidity and water saturation. (Photo courtesy of R.B. Pickering.)

Figure 13   In many parts of the U.S., chenopodium is a volunteer plant that indicates recent soil disturbance. (Photo courtesy of R.B. Pickering.)

can help you identify the volunteer plants in your area that may be helpful in identifying disturbed ground even when it is covered with plant growth.

The habits of animals or birds can provide clues to the location of a remains, either on the surface or buried. Remains that have been left on the surface are likely to be scavenged by wild and domestic carnivores such as coyotes, wolves, and dogs. Once skeletonized, the remains also may be attacked by rodents. Even birds may play a part in the removal of certain parts of remains. Knowing the habits of these animals can be helpful. For example, birds may take hair as nesting material or shiny objects such as jewelry for the nest. Small bones may be taken into rodent burrows and later expelled on the dirt pile at the entrance to the burrow. It is not uncommon to find that ground hogs make burrows in ancient burial sites. Rodents also may be attracted to the loose soil in recent clandestine gravesites. The attraction of carnivores to recent remains is well documented. Any remains left on the ground surface or buried in a shallow grave is likely to be damaged by hungry animals. As part of any search, the investigator should examine the nests, lairs, and resting spots of animals and birds within the search area. Portions of remains and personal effects may be found in such places.

"Here's a Bone, We Have a Problem"

The second scenario in the discovery of remains involves someone actually bringing in a portion of a remains. The task then is to find the rest of it. In this case, the informant may be able to lead the investigator directly to the remains or at least to the spot where the recovered portion was found. Yet, there are times when the portion is not recovered at the actual site where the body has been deposited. Therefore, a broader search is required to find the remains. Again, the role of animals is often important.

A case involving a small dog provides a good example. Like many rural homes and businesses, a mechanics shop in Northern Illinois had a dog, a mixed breed weighing about 10 lbs. This farm dog was adept at chasing wildlife and sometimes brought back the carcasses to the fenced-in yard. This scavenging was known to the dog's owner and it was not a matter of concern until the day the dog tried to drag a human skull under the fence and into the yard. The skull, weighing about half as much as the dog, got stuck under the fence (Figure 14). At this point, the owners clearly recognized that something was amiss. Immediately, the owners called the local sheriff who in turn called the coroner's office. The coroner's office called a forensic anthropologist and within about 90 minutes the recovery crew of sheriff's deputies, coroner's officials, and an anthropologist converged on the site.

An examination of the skull revealed a number of important details. There was no doubt that the skull was human. Moreover, soft tissue and hair still adhered to the skull's surface. Although badly deteriorated, remnants of the brain were still inside. The first few neck (cervical) vertebrae were in their normal anatomical position at the base of the skull. Cursory examination revealed no obvious peri-mortem trauma. The dog had found the skull in

Figure 14 A skull with soft tissue still present was discovered by a small dog. This was the first clue that a search of the area needed to be initiated. (Photo courtesy of R.B. Pickering.)

mid-summer, a time of long, hot, and humid days in Northern Illinois. With the amount of soft tissue still adhering to the skull, it was determined that the time since death was a matter of weeks rather than months. Shortly after, time of death was verified the rest of the remains was recovered.

The discovery of the skull prompted the question, "Where is the rest of the body?" Dogs have fairly regular habits. Knowing something about those habits can help determine how the dog may have found the remains. For example, dogs often look for cool places to sleep in the afternoon heat. According to the owner, while this particular dog had free range over a large area outside the fenced yard, it always returned to rest. When asked to point out the spot, he quickly led the team to a grassy area near the garage that was shaded in the afternoon. A quick walk over the area revealed a large number of bone fragments scattered over about 4 × 6 m. Even this superficial examination revealed that most of the bone fragments were human (Figure 15). Using flagging pins obtained from the investigator, the anthropologist began marking the location of each bone fragment. Once all fragments were marked and photographed, they were collected. Although it was clear that virtually all fragments were human bone, it still was not clear whether just one or multiple bodies were represented. Therefore, the anthropologist made a log book giving each fragment a number and identified it by location and type of bone fragment. In this way it was possible to see if

Figure 15   Each flagging pin marks the location of a human bone fragment brought to the yard by the family's dog. (Photo courtesy of R.B. Pickering.)

there were duplicate remains which might represent multiple bodies. In fact, there was only one body present.

By having an anthropologist in the field, it was possible to record the pertinent data quickly and efficiently. During this part of the discovery, it was also possible for the anthropologist to think and make preliminary observations while still at the site. Two particularly important points emerged. First, the anthropologist was able to segregate the human remains from animal remains while in the field. The preliminary examination showed that virtually all of the bones were human and that only one individual was involved; determinations which help speed the investigation and keep it on track. More importantly, it determined that all of the fragments found were from the upper part of the body, e.g., the head, chest, and arms. Nothing from the pelvis or below was represented by even a single fragment.

Considering that the team now was faced with remnants of an upper torso, the obvious question was, "Where is the rest of the body?" Because the recovery site was about 200 m from a busy interstate and the intervening area was a field in waist-high grass and a few clumps of trees, the deputy predicted that the body had been dropped off along the highway. This conclusion was reasonable considering the not uncommon occurrence of such events over the years. The entire team fanned out over the field and for more than an hour walked, looked, and sweated through a systematic survey. Nothing was found.

The decision was made to return to the garage, call for more assistance, and return to the search. In the meantime, the people already assembled would continue to search. On a hunch, the anthropologist asked the owner where the dog slept and from which direction the wind blew during this time of the year. The reason for these seemingly strange questions was that the dog had found the body and unless the body was very near, the suspicion was that the dog must have smelled it first and then went looking for it. With a puzzled look on his face, the owner pointed out the direction of the wind and the anthropologist and one remaining deputy began walking in that direction. Shortly, a remnant of hair that might have belonged to the remains was found. After about a 15-min walk along the fence-row lined with scrub trees and high grass, the remains was found in a shallow pit. The dog had found the body and over a period of weeks had been digging it out and carrying portions away. Standing at the site of the pit, one could look back through the trees at the garage — no more than 100 m away — but in the opposite direction from the interstate where the body was initially thought to have been. Surprisingly, there was no great odor except at the edge of the pit where the body had been deposited. The tell-tale smell of a decaying corpse attracted the dog, but could not be detected at the garage or at the road just a few meters away. Walking a straight line back to the garage from the pit, other remnants of the body including the complete but disarticulated mandible were found. Apparently, the dog had taken the shortest line between two points to get back to the yard.

The point of this story is that decisions made in the field by the forensic anthropologist, who identified the skeletal elements on site and recognized patterns of behavior that led to their disposition in the yard, made it possible to conduct a recovery that was more rapid and efficient than would have been possible if the bones had been taken to the lab for analysis. Expertise in the field leads to rapid decisions that may not only save time but also may reveal more details about the circumstances of the remains and their disposition.

The third scenario involves the forensic anthropologist being presented with a box of bones and asked to provide as many details as possible about the remains. In such cases, the anthropologist can determine the biological characteristics of the remains but, by not seeing the remains where they were found, may not be able to reconstruct much of the context (Figure 16). However, the bones themselves do carry clues about their context as two actual cases will help explain.

The anthropologist received a call saying that some boys had brought some bones to school for show and tell. The teacher recognized that the bones were human and called the police. Upon questioning, the boys said that they had walked to school through a cemetery in a large urban community. In

Figure 16 A box of bones delivered to the lab is a typical case for forensic anthropologists. While many biological details can be determined, more data can be gained when the anthropologist is part of the recovery team. (Photo courtesy of R.B. Pickering.)

cities, cemeteries do not have much room to expand; therefore, they sometimes "stack" caskets, meaning they excavate a series of graves to a greater depth than normal. A casket is then placed in the bottom of the deep hole, dirt is added and another casket is placed in the hole, and finally the grave is filled in. The detectives determined that the cemetery in question recently had finished an extensive project of this type. Apparently, they were not as tidy about re-interring remains as might be expected. When the boys walked through the cemetery, they picked up bones found on the ground and took them to school.

The anthropologist was asked to determine the age and sex of the bones so that they might be reinterred in the proper grave. Within a few hours, the detective delivered a box of bones and asked, "Who is it?" The most obvious bone was a complete skull with a gold crown and evidence of a number of ante-mortem dental extractions. The bone still was a bit greasy. A cursory examination showed that the skull belonged to a female, probably a small person, who at minimum, was in her late 50s. While looking at the rest of the bones in the box a large femur that appeared to be from an adult male was discovered. It did not seem to go with the skull. It was only after all the bones had been laid out that the shocking complexity of the case became apparent. There were four femurs representing four different people: an adult male, a female, and two children of different ages. What initially looked like a simple case suddenly had become more complicated and required a better explanation, particularly from the cemetery association.

Although the detective in the cemetery case needed only a few facts about the bones, there are many cases in which the anthropologist is asked to provide much more detailed information from a box of bones. Colorado, like many states, is known for its natural beauty which attracts many campers, hikers, and immigrants from other states who want to enjoy nature. As more people explore remote areas, there are more accidents and more people die from falls, exposure, or any number of other causes. There are homicides, too. Remains are found in remote areas by hikers, hunters, and foresters. They sometimes collect the bones and bring them to the local ranger or sheriff, thinking they are providing a service. In this situation, the anthropologist receives the bones but little other useful information.

Unlike the cemetery case, in cases like the one described the coroner wants to know everything about the remains. Is there evidence of trauma? When did this person die? Who is it? Determining the biological characteristics in this kind of case is no different from other cases. However, if the remains has been collected by amateurs it is rare that all of the bones are found. Two main factors are responsible: first, the recoverers may not recognize human bone, particularly if it is fragmented and second, remains in remote areas are commonly disturbed by animals. If there are large carnivores such as bears, mountain lions, wolves, or coyotes, the damage and loss may be severe (Figure 17). In these instances the anthropologist works with whatever remains are recovered and usually can determine the major biological categories of age, sex, race, and height. If present, other kinds of unusual bony changes can be identified by the anthropologist. However, an incomplete skeleton means incomplete data and description.

Even when a remains is incomplete the anthropologist still may be able to answer some questions about context which may be used to determine time since death. However, this is one of the most difficult questions to answer for any investigator because there are so many variables that affect it. If the anthropologist has not been at the site, it is helpful to have the anthropologist and the investigator talk to the recovery team to glean any details that might help bracket the time in which death may have occurred. Important questions will include: Was the body dressed or covered with any other material? What kind of soil or other material was under the body? Was it in direct sunlight or was it shaded under trees? Were the bones all together, "like a skeleton," or were they scattered in any way? While this list is not exhaustive it shows that a detailed description of the recovery site is needed. If the anthropologist cannot do it firsthand, then it needs to be reconstructed through bones, evidence, photos, and questions.

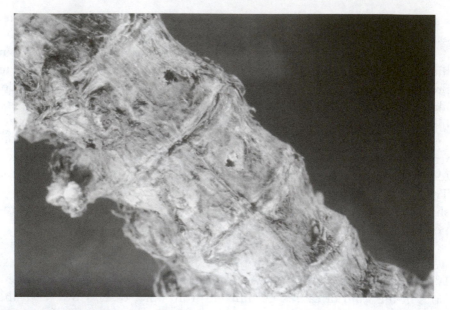

Figure 17 Puncture wounds and gnawing marks are typical damage on bones and bodies made by large carnivores such as dogs, wolves, and coyotes. (Photo courtesy of R.B. Pickering.)

This last scenario makes an important point: all forensic cases require detailed data gathering at the scene and in the lab. When skeletons are involved, forensic anthropologists can gather more data more efficiently than can people who are not trained to work with bones. In the long run, bringing the anthropologist to the field can save time, money, and headaches.

The Forensic Anthropologist and Recovery of Remains

There is no unimportant link in the chain of events related to the identification of human remains. However, the actual recovery of the remains and recording of the information at the recovery site provides the data for all subsequent analysis and interpretation. Without complete recovery and accurate and detailed descriptions, an accurate reconstruction of events is not possible.

A forensic anthropologist, particularly one who also has training and experience in archaeology, can be a valuable asset at the recovery site. The goal of good recovery is to record the relationships between the remains, the personal effects, other evidentiary materials, and the natural surroundings so that the disposal event can be reconstructed. Just picking up bones and personal effects does not constitute good recovery. While a detailed recovery may answer some questions, it is the relationship between remains and objects that reveals the events and behavior that occurred. More succinctly, the goal is to answer the questions: "Why is this remains here?" and "How did it come to be?" The systematic identification of which objects are cultural and which ones are natural, and the recording of these observations in writing and photo images is essential. To confuse a piece of evidence as being caused by a person when it was a natural change due to climatic conditions, scavengers, or other natural processes can be misleading as well as embarrassing, particularly when it is revealed by someone else.

One hypothetical and two actual cases provide useful examples. For the hypothetical case, we can assume that the probable place where a body was buried has been found. There is a depression in the dirt, the ground obviously has been disturbed, and there are volunteer plants growing (Figure 18). If the remains is indeed buried in this spot, the next step is to carefully excavate and document what you find without causing any destruction of the remains or evidence. If the remains is not there, you want to find out quickly, without wasting a lot of time or effort, and move on.

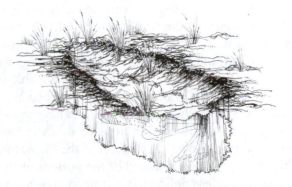

Figure 18   A depression in the ground with soft, loose dirt and a scattering of volunteer plants may indicate a clandestine grave. (Drawing courtesy of L. Schulz-kump, M.D.)

One method that allows for careful yet rapid and efficient excavation is as follows. The area around the presumed grave, at least 2 m on all sides of the grave, should be cordoned off for security. Photos should be taken of the ground surface as found so that your reasons for excavating can be documented. Any vegetation and leaf litter should then be scraped or raked away. Even this surface debris should be examined in detail for any evidentiary material. With the vegetation removed, the ground surface is exposed. If a clandestine grave has been excavated recently, the surface of the ground may be different from the surrounding ground. The soil may be softer and not

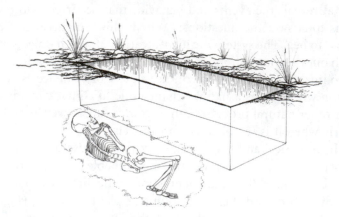

Figure 19 Stage 1 is the excavation of a rectangular trench along one side of the burial pit. (Drawing courtesy of L. Schulzkump, M.D.)

densely packed. The color of the soil also may differ from the surrounding undisturbed soil.

If a pit can be defined on the ground surface, it is likely that the remains is directly below. The worst method of excavation is to dig directly down through the pit to the skeleton. Almost without doubt, this method will break bones or objects and will make the process of excavation difficult. The preferred method is to lay out a rectangle along one long side of the pit (Figure 19). As this rectangle is excavated, it will be possible to see the side of the pit and to tell what part of the earth is undisturbed and which part is the fill within the pit. Very likely, this rectangle will have to be excavated no more than a few feet in depth. However, to make sure you have reached the bottom of the pit and for the physical comfort of the excavators while working, digging this rectangle below the level of the bottom of the pit is useful.

Once the long rectangle is finished, it is time to excavate a narrow, short rectangle along one of the short ends of the pit (Figure 20). If you think you know which is the head and which is the foot end, choose the foot end first. As the excavation nears the bottom of the pit, care needs to be taken not to disturb anything. At this point, the purpose is to find the precise location of the skeleton. Uncovering it comes later.

After the first short rectangle is excavated, then a short rectangle can be excavated at the other short end of the pit (Figure 21). This procedure lets the excavators know exactly where the skeleton is lying. Knowing this in advance makes the rest of the excavation go faster and more efficiently. In addition, by working on the skeleton from the side, the chances of breaking something are much reduced and the ability to map things exactly as found is greatly enhanced. In short, this technique will give you more information faster than digging down on the skeleton from the top.

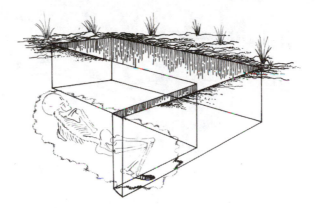

Figure 20   Stage 2 of the excavation extends a narrow trench at one end of the pit to find the feet. (Drawing courtesy of L. Schulzkump, M.D.)

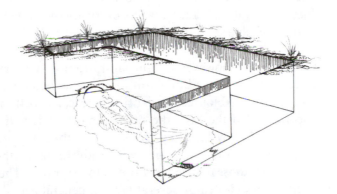

Figure 21   Stage 3 of the excavation extends the pit along the other end of the burial pit to find the head. (Drawing courtesy of L. Schulzkump, M.D.)

The final excavation stage (Figure 22) involves turning the three small rectangles into one large rectangle that reveals the remains. The space allows for clear mapping and photography, it gives workers enough space to move around, and it clearly shows the exact locations and relationships of objects and bones.

Let's take a look at a second case, only in this one the local coroner, police, or sheriff recover a skeletal remains and take the bones to an anthropologist. The remnants of clothing and other personal effects and objects go to the crime lab. The anthropologist can determine from the bones the biological characteristics of the person such as age, sex, height, and possibly ante- and peri-mortem trauma. The crime lab personnel might find and identify bullets, parts of clothing, or other objects; however, they may not

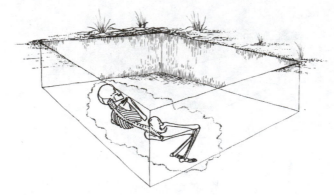

Figure 22 Stage 4 of the excavation removes all of the soil over the remains to allow easy mapping, photography, and removal of the skeleton. (Drawing courtesy of L. Schulzkump, M.D.)

know the relationship of these objects to the actual skeleton. If the anthropologist conducts a careful excavation and recovery, the relationship of personal effects and other objects to the skeleton can be clearly demonstrated. Figure 23 shows a skeletal case in which clothing was found but much of the fabric had disintegrated. However, as the anthropologist excavated the remains in place, the presence and position of clothing could be seen, e.g., the body was fully clothed in blouse, bra, panties, blue jeans, socks, and shoes.

The more complicated the case, the more important it is to have the anthropologist at the site. By knowing the skeleton, the anthropologist is thinking about the relationship of bones with indications of the normal deterioration process vs. those induced by human intervention. The recovery of a remains can be complicated by several factors: general age of the individual (infant, juvenile, adult), the number of individuals, and intentional attempts to destroy the remains. For example, a single, fully skeletonized remains with all bones present and in anatomical position is much easier to recover and examine than are commingled remains.

The remains of infants and juveniles are a greater challenge, because in the very young, bones are not only smaller than those of adults but also have different forms. At birth, long bones such as the humerus are not one single bone (Figure 24). They consist of a shaft (diaphysis) and growth centers (epiphyses) at each end. As the individual gets older, the shaft and ends grow together to make the complete bone. It is the regularity of this process that allows anthropologists to estimate age from juvenile bones. Unfortunately, the bones of the very young may not look human; they are a size that can be confused with the bones of some animals. Even more difficult is that while an inexperienced recovery may identify and retrieve the shafts of long bones, they may not recognize the growth centers that exist throughout the skeleton. There are even

Figure 23 Careful removal of the rocks and soil over the remains revealed the skeleton and the location of all items of evidence. (Photo courtesy of R.B. Pickering.)

cases where the normally unfused portions of bones have been confused with fractures; thereby, the normal condition was confused with trauma.

Remains that are not completely skeletonized present other kinds of problems. Partly decomposed bodies are unpleasant at best. In advanced stages of decomposition, internal organs may be completely gone. In such cases, the pathologist and toxicologist may have little to examine. Yet, even in an intermediate state of decomposition, it is necessary to examine all remains to determine whether the remains is complete and to determine if any culturally induced change has occurred, such as a gunshot, stab wound, or a blunt instrument strike. Figure 25 illustrates a remains that was badly decomposed and internal organs were virtually unidentifiable. In a case such as this, the physical anthropologist assisted the pathologist in extracting the maximum amount of data from a poorly preserved remains.

A case from Will County, IL, provides a good example. Remains were found in late winter on the edge of a stream. Most of the soft tissue had

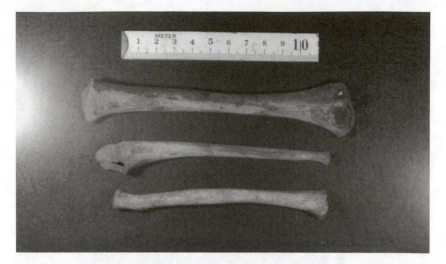

Figure 24   The skeleton of a fetus or a newborn looks very different from the skeleton of an adult. (Photo courtesy of R.B. Pickering.)

Figure 25   Remains in advanced stages of decomposition offer special challenges to the pathologist and the forensic anthropologist. (Photo courtesy of R.B. Pickering.)

decomposed except for the left foot and lower leg which had been submerged in the cold water of the winter stream. Here the skin and other soft tissues were relatively well preserved. Some burning had been noted on an area of the chest and on an arm (Figure 26). In these areas, both soft tissue and bone

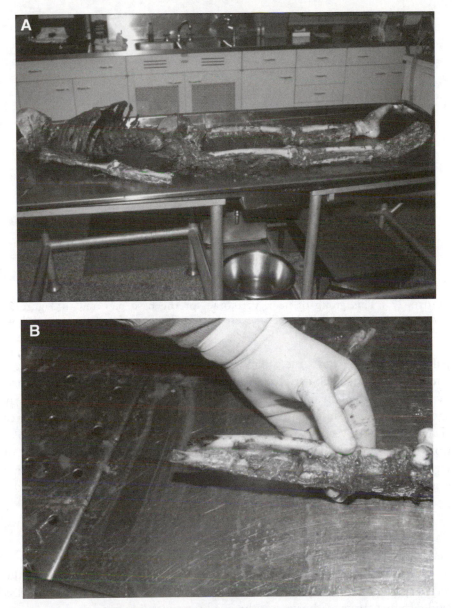

Figure 26 (A) Although the soft tissue still covers part of the remains, the forensic anthropologist conducts a complete inventory of all bones. (B) Detailed examination reveals changes to the body, some of which may be natural and others that may be related to the crime. (Photos courtesy of R.B. Pickering.)

had been burned. The remains appeared to be mostly complete, except for hands, which were missing. The broken ends and partial burning of the bones of the forearm indicated that they had been traumatically severed. The forensic anthropologist conducted a complete inventory of bones in the lab. While

Figure 27   This group of neck vertebrae for the case pictured in Figure 26 revealed that the head had been severed from the body from the rear. (Photo courtesy of R.B. Pickering.)

palpating the neck vertebrae, small sharp splinters and bone fragments were encountered. The neck vertebrae were removed from the body and cleaned by simmering them in an enzyme action detergent solution. The result clearly showed that the head, like the hands, had been severed from the body. Once cleaned, the neck vertebrae were placed in anatomical position and the position of the cut could be seen (Figure 27). Determination of the type of weapon used and the direction from which the blow was delivered also were done. In this case, the examination added considerable detail about how the perpetrator had attempted to alter the body.

Attempts to disguise or destroy remains also cause identification problems. The more determined the attempt, the greater the difficulty. However, even major destruction of bone still can yield information about the deceased and the event of death. In these kinds of cases, having the anthropologist at the recovery site is absolutely crucial. Perhaps a truism of analysis is that the less evidence that survives, the greater the need for specialists from the beginning.

Attempts to destroy remains by fire are not uncommon, whether by starting a fire to cover up a murder or intentionally trying to incinerate the body itself. The example below gives insight into this problem.

This case involves murder and the intentional effort to dispose of a remains. A few fragments of bone had been sent to the state crime lab (Colorado Bureau of Investigation). At the lab director's request, the anthropologist examined the bone and identified it as human and as a portion of the lower forearm. On that basis, he was asked by the coroner and sheriff's detectives to fly to a remote part of the state and recover a burned remains. The remains were found in a backyard barbecue pit that had been excavated out of the soil and lined with medium-sized boulders. Inside the pit could be seen the ash and charcoal that would be expected as a result of any cookout. However, on close examination of the pit, particularly near the sides, badly burned but identifiable human bone and tooth fragments could be seen.

In consultation with the staff of the sheriff and coroner, the recovery team quickly created a plan for recovery. The sheriff had asked a local university archaeologist and one of her students to come to the site in case help might be needed. Because of her training, the archaeologist was a great asset in mapping and recording our observations.

With trowel and small brushes, the anthropologist began to excavate the contents of the pit. By working from the side of the pit that had the least concentration of remains toward the higher concentrations, it was possible to quickly isolate the area in which the bones were to be found. In addition, excavation was done in layers; each layer being a different color or density of charcoal debris or soil. The entire excavation was completed in one day and resulted only in a small box of remains and evidentiary objects. However, recording the relationship of these pieces of data in the field helped reconstruct some details surrounding the disposal of the body. For example, it was possible to determine that even though a high percentage of the actual bone had been destroyed, portions representing virtually all sections of the body, such as the head, vertebrae, arms, hands, pelvis, legs, and feet were found. The position of the body in the pit as it was being burned was discernible. The careful excavation also revealed fragments of the deceased's watch and footgear. Most important was the discovery of a small fragment of mandible with a single ante-mortem tooth loss and a dental appliance that matched the mandible fragment. Indeed, this find was the primary means of identifying the victim. Careful recovery of even tiny fragments made it possible to reconstruct teeth and bones in the lab. For example, (Figure 28) most of a humerus was reconstructed from more than 25 fragments. In some cases, teeth were reconstructed from as many as four fragments.

Field Recovery

Efficient recovery of remains from the field requires:

1. Preplanning of equipment needs
2. An ability to read soil disturbances that may indicate where a body is buried

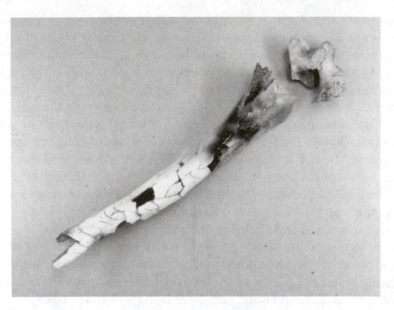

Figure 28   Remains recovered from fire or explosion sites may require reconstruction as part of the analysis. This partial humerus was reconstructed from more than 20 fragments. (Photo courtesy of R.B. Pickering.)

3. An understanding of how animals may disturb burials and damage bones
4. The ability to excavate buried bones without disturbing their relationship or damaging them

The Final Report

All forensic specialists understand the importance of clear, concise, and comprehensive recordkeeping; you should expect no less from a consulting anthropologist. Any report submitted should be the result of your consultation with the anthropologist and in the format and style that is agreeable to both parties. The style of the report or portion of the report that describes the recovery of remains also should be agreed upon in advance. Discuss the kinds of maps and imaging, still photography, and video that you expect.

The report should be clearly labeled with a case number provided by the office, either the coroner or medical examiner, that requests the anthropologist's services. This point may sound obvious but it is a common problem because different agencies, and even the anthropologists themselves, may have their own numbering system to keep track of cases. Therefore because each system is likely to be different, careful attention must be given to make sure that each case is clearly identified. A list of anthropological personnel who participated in the case and their roles also should be given. For example, some people may have helped on only one or a few parts of the process. The list should identify who actually excavated material, who screened, who drew maps, took photos, etc.

In addition to the personnel, there should be a listing or outline of the procedures used. For example, was excavation by trowel, shovel, or a combination of techniques. Was the debris screened? If so, what width mesh screen was used? Procedures describing the removal, bagging, and marking of objects should be provided as well.

The graphic section of the report should include a basic plan and cross-section view maps of the recovery site. If the recovery site is complex, additional detailed maps may be needed. At least one version of the site map should pinpoint the location of each bone or bone fragment and each artifact (evidentiary item), identifying each find by a code number. Those numbers should be keyed to an inventory that defines every item that was taken out of the ground and saved.

A set of photos should be taken that includes views of the recovery site from various directions and distances. These views will assist in placing the discovery site in its context. Next, photos of the remains as it was found should be taken. If excavation is required, then photos at different stages of the excavation should be made to show the relationship of remains and objects that might be overlapping. The anthropologist will take close-up photos of each section of the remains. These images provide crucial verification of important pieces of evidence or relationships between objects and remains. A copy of these images should be required as part of the report. A video record is a valuable tool for recording the process as well as the results of recovery. However, if the anthropologist is doing the recovery, someone else will have to be the videographer. The most prudent course of action is to use multiple techniques to record the scene. For this approach to be most effective, however, the team must decide in advance who is responsible for each kind of recording.

Things You Can Do to Make Recovery Easier

1. Decide on necessary equipment and personnel and who will provide them before starting the recovery.
2. Get expert help if the location of the remains is not evident.
3. Use a forensic anthropologist to assist in field recovery to obtain more complete information about the case.
4. Use excavation techniques that are not going to damage the remains or evidence.
5. Discuss the information required in final reports prior to beginning investigation.

Ten Key Questions

5

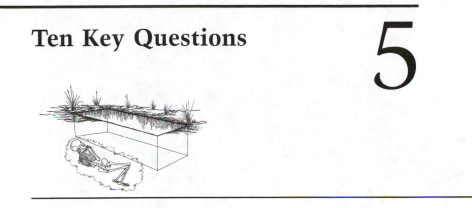

Each time you are responsible for investigating a report of possible skeletal remains, you know that you will be facing a situation with many unknowns. To simplify your task, a series of ten key questions must be answered in order for you to complete a thorough forensic investigation. The answers to these questions rarely are obvious enough to let you close your case quickly. In most cases the only way to get accurate answers to these questions is to seek outside help. If you find a recently dead person only partially decomposed or in cases where most or all soft tissue is gone, you will need the help of a forensic anthropologist to answer your questions.

The first in this series of 10 questions will determine if this is a forensic case or, more properly, if it fits in the domain of historians or archaeologists, for example, an ancient Native American burial. The remaining questions describe specific biological characteristics of the remains that may help identify both the remains and the circumstances surrounding the death of this person.

Question #1: Is it bone?

All of us can recognize bones if we see a complete skeleton. Most of us can recognize intact bones. It becomes more difficult if we are faced with fragmented bones. Many common materials such as plastic or pieces of tree root have been confused with bone. Fragments of cortical bone have been confused with some types of foam insulation. Few of us are able to confidently identify cremated human bone. Bones are rarely completely consumed by fire, but burned bones will be badly broken and deformed and their color and texture changed. This makes detection difficult and only someone experienced in bone identification will be able to tell if bones are present at a burn scene.

Figure 29   A forensic anthropologist should participate in the recovery phase of a case, particularly those which involve explosion and fire. (Photo courtesy of R.B. Pickering.)

In the early 1980s, the Union Oil Refinery of Romeoville, IL, experienced a disastrous explosion and fire which claimed more than 10 victims. At the time the anthropologist was called in on the case, all but one had been identified. Finally, a fragment was found which was identified by the pathologist as a skull fragment which should have represented the final unidentified victim. The anthropologist's task was to excavate and examine the area around the fragment and to find the rest of the remains. Aided by the staff at the refinery and from the coroner's office and armed with trowel and shovel, he began to excavate in the muck. The area in which he worked was covered by petroleum product, chemicals, and debris from the explosion. Needless to say, it was a difficult environment in which to work (Figure 29). After more than half a day of systematically troweling many small identifiable objects, only bolts, washers, and pencils were found. However, nothing identifiable as bone was evident. After a few more hours of frustrating excavation, the anthropologist began to have some doubts. While he had initially accepted the determination of the pathologist that the fragment was part of a human cranial vault, he now asked to see the actual specimen. Either the fire and explosion had been so intense that the body had been totally incinerated, or the fragment was not really bone.

The coroner's official arranged to have the specimen brought to the site within an hour. The piece was wrapped and protected in a small jar. Upon unwrapping it, it was evident that it was the right thickness and had a curve that made it look like human cranial vault. There was only one problem, it

Figure 30 Initially, this object was identified as human bone. Later it was identified by the anthropologist and a petrologist as plastic. (Photo courtesy of R.B. Pickering.)

was not bone; it was plastic (Figure 30). This rather disturbing conclusion created a dilemma. This case was the first one on which the anthropologist had worked for this particular coroner. The pathologist who had misidentified the fragment had worked for the county for 20 years. Who was the coroner to believe? The team continued to work at the site for another entire day without finding any remains. The fragment was shown to a petroleum geologist who also identified it as plastic. Sadly, no remains of the final victim were found. However, if the question, "Is it bone?" had been asked and answered initially this whole exercise could have been avoided.

Question #2: Is it human?

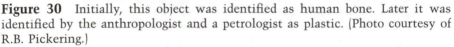

Again, anyone will recognize a skeleton that has the bones lying in a normal anatomical configuration. If soft tissue or hair is still present you can feel even more confident that you are dealing with human remains. Scattered bones present a more difficult problem. You'll be able to identify a human skull; its rounded vault and flat face distinguish human from animal skulls. A cross-section of cranial vault bone differs significantly from turtle shell — another type of bone sometimes confused with human skull fragments. If you find teeth with dental work, fillings or caps, you can be pretty certain they are human. People lavish a lot of money and attention on their pets, but it would be a rare veterinarian that will fill a dog's teeth.

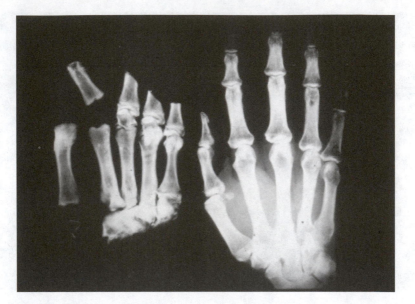

Figure 31   Some animal bones can be confused with human bones. The bones on the left are a bear's paw, the hand on the right is human. (Photo courtesy of C.C. Snow.)

Other bones like the vertebrae, ribs, long bones, pelvis, and small bones of the hands and feet present a more difficult problem. These bones, in both humans and animals, have similar characteristics and some experience is needed to tell them apart. Bones from a bear's paws, front and back, often have been mistakenly identified as human hands (Figure 31). Human and deer vertebrae are similar in size and appearance. Skeletal remains that still have some flesh on them can be more confusing. It is difficult to tell what bone you are dealing with if it is still partly covered with muscle.

Bones of young children and infants will confuse almost everyone. Fetal bones and those of newborns are even more difficult as they are small and few of us are used to seeing bones that size. Additionally, the form of juvenile bones is different from adult bones. Growth centers (epiphyses) separate the ends of long bones from their shafts (Figure 32). These growth centers fuse to the shaft at different times during development but, because of the ununited epiphyses, there will appear to be an excessive number of bones in children's skeletons. Unless a person is trained to identify these bones and has worked with them these determinations are especially difficult.

If the bones are fragmented or burned even an expert will have initial trouble distinguishing pieces of human bones from pieces of animal bones. A forensic anthropologist can make that determination but it requires training, experience, and time.

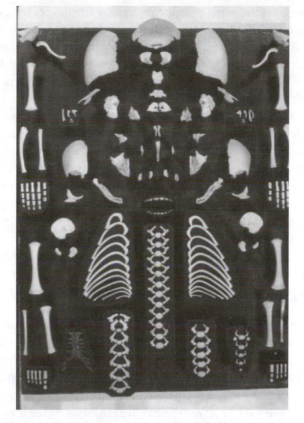

Figure 32 Human infant skeletons include many more elements than an adult skeleton and they are small and delicate. Great care is needed to completely recover and identify bones form the very young. (Photo courtesy of R.B. Pickering.)

Question #3: Is it modern?

Are these skeletal remains from an ancient burial, more than 100 years old, or are they from a recently deceased person and of forensic interest? Determining time since death is one of the most difficult questions to answer because so many variables affect decomposition of a body. If the discovered remains are found on the surface of the ground and skin and hair are still present on the remains, you know that this death was relatively recent. Buried remains, particularly in a coffin or wrapped in protective material such as heavy plastic, will also preserve soft tissue for a long time, which makes time since death difficult to determine.

Lt. Colonel William M. Shy, 20th Tennessee, was killed in the Battle of Nashville on December 18, 1864. In December 1977, his grave, located in the backyard of a Nashville home, was disturbed and skeletal remains were found.

On first impression the remains appeared to be from a recent death because of the odor and pink flesh that was still present on the bones that were found in the coffin. Authorities were certain that Colonel Shy's remains would have completely decomposed. The initial opinion was that these remains were only 6–8 months old. Further investigation showed that these were the remains of Colonel Shy whose body had been embalmed and buried in a coffin. Embalming and coffin burials slow decomposition.

Fully skeletonized remains are an even more difficult problem. Sometimes, morphological features such as shovel-shaped incisors common to ancient Native American skeletons can be used to differentiate ancient and modern remains. They occur with high frequency among Native American populations, ancient and modern. In fact, they occur frequently in all mongoloid populations. Shovel-shaped incisors are quite rare but not unknown among caucasoids and negroids, thus making the trait a useful one.

Another trait that sometimes can be used to separate modern and ancient remains is the amount of bowing of the femur. For example, ancient peoples did not use furniture as we do today. To rest, they squatted. This same posture is still common in many parts of the world. However, in the U.S., most of us sit or recline on chairs and sofas when we rest. Resting postures as well as work-related activities affect the bone. People who squat tend to have bowed femurs while people who do not tend to have relatively straight ones (Figure 33). These two traits represent an important rule: while a trait may suggest a race or age for a remains virtually no trait can be used alone. An anthropologist will look at all morphological features to see if they are useful.

Artifacts discovered with the remains also can give evidence about whether a remains is ancient or modern. If a stone axe, arrowheads, and bone beads are found with the remains, it is probably an ancient burial. If you find 1990 coins with the remains you have another clue. Remnants of clothing will give you a hint of when this subject lived. Buckskin clothing is most often associated with ancient remains although don't bet on that; modern fashion has rediscovered buckskin. An Armani label should give you a hint that this is a recent death.

Make certain that the remains agree with the artifacts. Maybe someone discovered a grave robber, decided to exact the ultimate penalty for that crime, and killed and buried the thief right on the spot. In other words, you could find skeletal remains right next to some ancient artifacts, but that would not mean that they were buried at the same time.

The insect population around remains often can give a hint as to how long these remains have been present at the site where they were discovered. Only an entomologist will be able to accurately determine the significance of insect findings.

Dental changes are important. Severe tooth wear and attrition into the dentin are usually associated with prehistoric cultures in most parts of the U.S. Dental repair and reconstruction indicate a more recent demise but that

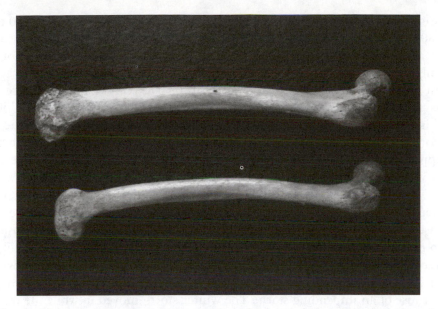

Figure 33 The femur on top is straight. The lower femur is curved along its length. Such subtle changes can be helpful to the anthropologist in identification. (Photo courtesy of Rick Wicker/DMNH.)

still leaves a wide span of time. An odontologist, particularly one who teaches at a dental school, may be able to tell the age of the restoration from its style. That clue may help determine the era in which the individual lived but will not necessarily help determine time since death. Even an expert may not be able to give you a definite date. There is an important statistic to remember: less than 50% of the U.S. population sees a dentist each year, so not everyone has had dental X-rays made in the past.

The process of identifying one set of remains found on the side of a mesa in Southwestern Colorado is instructive. It appeared that erosion due to runoff from snow and rain had exposed a human skull and some ribs. Because the burial was on a steep incline in an unpopulated area, and because the bones were buried directly in the ground, it was assumed that these remains were ancient Native American. In this circumstance, Colorado law requires investigation and recovery by the state archaeologist. He agreed that this was an ancient burial. When the remains were excavated and recovered our suspicion was confirmed. One of the buried ribs had an arrowhead embedded in it. This was an ancient burial dating from 1000 to 1600 A.D.

We could have dated this more specifically by having the bones carbon 14 (^{14}C) tested. The unstable isotope of carbon, ^{14}C, is present in every living organism. At death, carbon 14 begins to decay at a predictable rate and by measuring the remaining amount of the isotope you can determine an accurate measurement of the time since the death of the organism. While that is useful in proving that a skeleton is ancient, it is also expensive, from $150 to $800 per test, and most agencies do not have a budget that permits dating of ancient bones. Moreover, ^{14}C is capable of determining the age of bone only within a specific range. For example, it can be used to determine age on organic material that is less than about 65,000 years of age or as recent as about 150 years. Outside of that range, ^{14}C dating is not reliable. While this technique is useful to archaeologists, it does not answer forensic questions. At this writing, there is no independent dating procedure which is appropriate for measuring time since death if it occurred within a few years or a few decades of the present time.

The time frame of most forensic cases frequently covers hours, days, or weeks. Months or a few years are usually the limit of forensic significance. A case from the Rocky Mountain region gives an example of the process used to determine time since death for modern remains. A man decided to hike a jeep trail over a 13,000-ft pass between two Southwestern Colorado towns in the late fall. He did this in the face of strong cautions against this trip because of an impending storm. The winter storm moved in while the man was on the road, closing the road for the winter, and he was reported missing. In the spring when the road was reopened, skeletal remains of a male were found seated on the ground, leaning against a rock. His shirt, jacket, and shoes had been removed and were neatly piled beside him. This behavior pointed to the conclusion that he had died of hypothermia. The fact that this body had not been spotted when jeeps were regularly crossing this pass in the fall was evidence that this was a recent death. Dental records positively identified this skeleton as that of the missing man. This case could be closed without notification of the state archaeologist because it was a forensic case with a natural cause of death.

Recent changes in the law, both state and federal, may affect the way you handle ancient skeletal remains. Colorado statutes require any person who discovers suspected human remains on any land to notify the coroner and law enforcement authorities. In the past six or seven years all 50 states have passed laws that define the procedure for treatment of historic remains. In Colorado the coroner, along with appropriate law enforcement agencies, must examine all remains within 48 hours to determine if they are human and, if so, to assess their forensic value. If these people are unable to do so, a forensic anthropologist must be called to assist in that determination. If it is determined that the remains do not constitute a forensic case then the Colorado state archaeologist must be notified. The state archaeologist will have the remains examined to determine if they are greater than 100 years old. If the remains are determined to be Native American, the state archaeologist must notify the Commission of Indian Affairs. The remains will be disinterred unless the state archaeologist and the chairman of the Commission of Indian Affairs agree to leave them *in situ*.

Once the remains have been disinterred, the state archaeologist may assume custody for one year for study and analysis. A physical anthropological study must be done and must include osteometric measurements, pathological analysis, age, sex, and cause of death determinations. At the completion of this study the state archaeologist must consult with the Commission of Indian Affairs regarding the site of reinterment of the remains. If the remains are shown to be non-Native American, they are to be conveyed to the Colorado State Anatomical Board.

If the remains are determined to be modern then you must proceed on the assumption that you are dealing with a forensic case and continue your investigation by answering the next question.

NAGPRA

A new Federal law applies to ancient remains. In 1990, President Bush signed the Native American Graves Protection and Repatriation Act (NAGPRA) into law. The NAGPRA law was written to protect ancient remains, but it has legal implications for all coroners and medical examiners. In the past, if remains were determined to be ancient and Native American, the coroner or medical examiner had no further legal responsibility. Now, discovery of ancient, Native American remains, whether the discovery is accidental or intentional, constitutes "new discovery" under the NAGPRA law. If such remains are brought to your attention, you must contact the State Historic Preservation Office (SHPO) or the state archaeologist to determine how to proceed. If you do not know that individual, they can usually be identified through the state museum or an archaeologist at the nearest college or university.

The law is intended to protect Native American burial sites and to control the removal of human remains, funerary objects, and items of cultural patrimony still located in archaeological sites on federal and tribal lands. The best advice is not to remove anything from a site but to immediately call the SHPO or state archaeologist. They will know how to proceed and they also will notify the appropriate tribal representatives. Removing any bones or associated artifacts may result in criminal prosecution under the Archaeological Resource Protection Act.

Another Federal law, NAGPRA has additional implications for federal agencies and museums receiving federal funds. They must inventory individual human remains and associated funerary objects and develop written summaries of unassociated funerary objects, sacred objects, and objects of cultural patrimony that are in the collections they control. They must make an attempt to identify the likely cultural affiliation of these items and notify the presumptive Native American organization and offer them the opportunity to claim the remains and cultural items.

Question #4: What bones are present?

Answering this question requires knowledge of human osteology. After the scene investigation is complete, your job is to make certain that all the bones have been collected. If all the bones are not recovered, your investigation may be missing an important bit of information that could resolve the case. Every bone may give a clue to who this person was and what circumstances lead to the remains being discovered there. As part of your case file, make certain that an inventory of the bones is done so you can be sure that all the bones are present. One of the often missed bones is the hyoid, which is so frequently broken in strangulation and so infrequently broken in any other manner.

Two cases found within several weeks of each other in the same jurisdiction illustrate this point. Two badly decomposed bodies were brought into the county morgue. Even though the bodies were 60–80% decomposed, the bones had to be inventoried. In both of these cases, the inventory revealed that bones, including the hyoid, were missing. A forensic anthropologist was sent with a detective to search the areas again and the missing elements, including the hyoid, were found. In one case, an ossified thyroid cartilage was found to have a definite fracture. Because the second search was delayed this finding could not be entered into evidence even though it pointed to strangulation as the cause of death. Had that fractured cartilage been found on the initial search and recovery, it would have been part of the case file as evidence.

Identification of the bones should be done by an expert, either the medical examiner or an anthropologist. Their expertise is vital, especially when viewed in the context of the next question.

Question #5: Is there more than one person present?

Humans have a definite number of bones and many of them are paired. There are pairs of arm bones and pairs of leg bones. You have 24 ribs — 12 on each side, 24 vertebrae plus a sacrum which is usually made up of five fused vertebrae, a coccyx, one pelvis consisting of the right and left innominates, and one skull. If you suddenly come up with an extra set of any of these bones you have a problem; your subject had a friend and your investigation has just become more complicated. The question of whether you have more than one body becomes more critical and difficult to answer if the bones are fragmented. Only an expert will be able to determine that three fragments of bone came from three different tibias. Three tibias mean at least two different people, maybe three, are present. If you have a bunch of bones coming from a number of individuals an experienced forensic anthropologist will be able to distinguish which bones belong to which individual and make a determination of how many individuals are represented.

An example from the Vietnam War years illustrates this point. Near Christmas of 1975, a number of skeletonized remains of American POWs who had died in captivity were returned by the North Vietnamese to the U.S. Army CIL in Thailand. Each remains was fully skeletonized and had been placed in a small, nicely made wooden box. On each box was a name, purported to be the name of the person whose remains were inside. Even with the name association, each remains was examined by an anthropologist who did not have knowledge of the biological characteristics of the individuals. Working separately, the civilian identification specialists within the lab used the names on the boxes to assemble medical and dental records to develop a biological profile for comparison.

Each remains was laid out on a separate examination table. A complete skeletal inventory was conducted and all bones were placed in normal anatomical position. All the bones had been cleaned by the North Vietnamese and appeared to have been covered with a preservative. During this process, extra bones were noted. In a few cases, there were extra fingers. In one case, there was an extra, complete neck vertebra. None of the other skeletons were missing a neck vertebra. Clearly, these bones, and especially the neck vertebra, represented an additional person, totally unaccounted for by the complete skeletons and associated names. Although this single additional bone could not be associated with an individual, it did point out that the remains had been commingled and that, eventually, the North Vietnamese would have to account for that person, too.

Question #6: What is the race, ethnicity, or cultural affiliation?

Race is both a cultural and a biological term. For more than a century scientists and philosophers have tried to define race and describe races. Some scientists define only three races: caucasoid, mongoloid, and negroid, while other scientists have defined more than ten. In our current climate of multicultural sensitivity some scholars, not forensic anthropologists, suggest that race does not exist, or at least it should not be talked about.

The dictionary gives several definitions for race. One definition is a local human population distinguished as a more or less distinct group by genetically transmitted physical characteristics. A second definition is any group of people united or classified together on the basis of a common history, nationality, or geographic distribution. In this definition, common history, religion, and other cultural characteristics supersede genetics. In any case, throughout the history of humanity there have been genetic patterns that vary in time and place. Even if one accepts the categorization defined by "race," there probably never was any such thing as a "pure" race. Wherever humans have gone, they have managed to successfully interbreed with any other group of humans encountered. Today, the ease and cheapness of travel mean that there are more people moving around the globe with greater genetic mixing than ever before.

From the forensic perspective, using the "three-race" model still has some value in describing broad genetic and morphological characteristics. This model is used by many people to describe themselves and others. Therefore, it falls to the forensic investigator to use the term defined by the model in trying to identify the dead. The model is not perfect, but it does help us understand some of the variation in shape and form on some parts of the skeleton, particularly the skull.

For the forensic anthropologist, determining race using the skull means looking at the shapes and relative sizes of some of the bones that form the facial features and some characteristics that contribute to the overall size and shape of the skull. Table 1 gives some of the characteristics used by anthropologists. However, every forensic anthropologist who has experience with skulls knows there are exceptions to this model. It is important to recognize that of all of the major biological variables, this one is perhaps the most difficult and easiest to misidentify. For this reason, your consulting anthropologist may not always be able to determine the race.

Table 1   Racial Characteristics of the Skull

Trait	Mongoloid	Caucasoid	Negroid
Skull length	Long	Short	Long
Skull breadth	Broad	Broad	Narrow
Skull height	Middle	High	Low
Sagittal contour	Arched	Arched	Flat
Face breadth	Very wide	Wide	Narrow
Face height	High	High	Low
Orbital opening	Rounded	Rounded	Rectangular
Nasal opening	Narrow	Mod. wide	Wide
Nasal bones	Wide, flat	Narrow, arched	Narrow
Lower nasal margin	Sharp	Sharp	Troughed
Facial profile	Straight	Straight	Downward slant
Palate shape	Mod. wide	Mod. wide	Wide
	Broad U-shape	V-shape	U-shape
Shovel-shaped incisors	90%+	<5%	<5%
General form	Large, smooth	Rounded large, rounded Mod. rugged	Smooth, elongated

Modified from Krogman, M. M., *The Human Skeleton in Forensic Medicine*, second edition, Charles C Thomas, Springfield, IL, 1973, pp. 129, 155, 190. With permission.

Figure 34 Detail of a skeletonized remains showing the location of deteriorated clothing and a plastic bag. (Photo courtesy of R.B. Pickering.)

Question #7: What is the sex?

Initially, clothing provides clues to the determination of sex, but these clues may be misleading. Definitive determination must be based on a skeletal examination. If you find that your subject was wearing a brassiere and a skirt you can usually, but not always, assume that you are dealing with a female (Figure 34). For identification of sex it is important to see the subject *in situ* before the remains are moved. In a case from Chicago, careful excavation revealed a body with the bra hooked and in place around the rib cage. The material of the jeans worn by the victim had disintegrated, but the piping down the side was intact and the zipper was zipped and in the normal position. The clothing suggested that the subject was female. If the clothing fragments had been picked up and brought to the lab without the chance of seeing them in place it would have been impossible to tell if the subject had been wearing the clothes or if they were simply incidental findings at the scene.

Unisex clothing has become popular and complicates identification. A flannel shirt and jeans will not separate males from females. Jewelry is often indicative of sex but with more males wearing earrings, jewelry is not as certain as it used to be. Other pieces of evidence such as pocket contents, handbags, wallets, etc., also may indicate the sex or possibly the identity of the deceased. However, even with proper analysis of evidence, determination of the sex still requires a detailed examination of the skeleton by a qualified anthropologist.

Determination of sex in adolescents and younger children ranges from difficult to impossible. Just as the external sexual changes do not become pronounced until adolescence, so too, the differences in the skeletons of young boys and girls are not pronounced until children begin to become adults. Determining sex from skeletons of children is based on measurements of numerous bones, particularly the long bones of the arms and legs and the bones of the pelvis. Essentially, all or most of the major bones must be present (Figure 35).

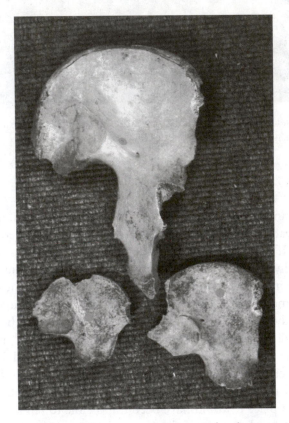

Figure 35   Bones of the pelvis are very important for determining age and sex. From childhood to adulthood, both size and shape change. (Photo courtesy of R.B. Pickering.)

Several elements of the skeleton can be used by a physical anthropologist to differentiate sex in adults, but the pelvis is the most reliable bony element. An expert can determine sex using the pelvis with about 90% accuracy, but a wise expert will not rely on just one skeletal element for that determination. The differences in the male/female pelvis reflect the basic biological difference

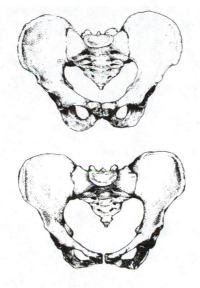

Figure 36 Top: the male pelvis has a smaller pelvic inlet and generally is narrower than the female pelvis. Bottom: the female pelvis has a broad, rounded pelvic inlet and a broader sacrum, relatively. (Drawings courtesy of L. Schulz-kump, M.D.)

between men and women; women bear children, men do not. From the skeletal perspective, the female pelvis tends to be broader and shorter than the male pelvis and the female pelvis has a relatively larger interior diameter than the male pelvis (Figure 36). Males tend to have a higher, narrower pelvis. A complicating feature is that sexual dimorphism — the difference in size and robusticity — varies from population to population. This point has forensic implications. For example, American blacks and American whites have a high degree of sexual dimorphism. The skeletons of males, generally, are noticeably larger and more robust than those of females. Therefore, seeing the skeletal differences is easier. However, among Southeast Asian populations, sexual dimorphism is less pronounced and the differences in bone sizes are not so different. As the American population includes more people from other parts of the world, specifically Southeast and South Asia, investigators need to be aware of these kinds of variations. A potential error could involve identifying a Southeast Asian male skeleton as an American female skeleton. Because of the population differences in sexual dimorphism, race or ethnicity must be determined *before* sex can be determined.

It is not unusual to have forensic and archaeological cases in which the determination of sex was not clear cut or the data seemed to be conflicting. Take the case of Wenu-hotep, the mummy of an ancient Egyptian who lived about 2500 years ago and now resides in a midwestern museum. According

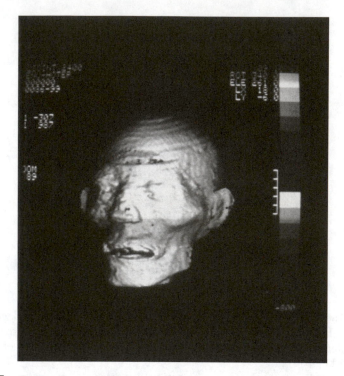

Figure 37   CAT scan reconstruction of the mummy Wenu-hotep suggests a face with a broad, masculine chin. However, soft tissue on the mummy definitely identified the sex as female. (Photo courtesy of R.B. Pickering.)

to hieroglyphs on the coffin, the mummy was female. However, in Egyptology checking to see if the mummy and the coffin actually go together is always necessary. Sometimes the ancient Egyptians put their relatives in other people's coffins and sometimes antiquity dealers put good mummies in good coffins to raise the selling price. On examining the full-body X-rays of Wenu-hotep, it was noted that the mandible was broad and the skull had a prominent brow ridge. Both these characteristics suggest that the person was male, not female (Figure 37). X-rays of the pelvis were inconclusive. Subjecting the wrapped mummy to CAT scan solved the problem. The pelvis presented clear female characteristics. Moreover, the CAT scan was capable of creating images of the soft tissue. The presence of desiccated breasts and lack of male genitalia clearly defined the sex. Although this case is archaeological, it demonstrates the need to look at all of the skeleton, not just one or a few features.

Table 2 identifies differences in the pelvis in males and females.

The skull is the next most reliable skeletal indicator of sex. Males tend to have larger and more rugged skulls than females. Usually, a large supraorbital ridge, long and broad mastoid processes, and a rugged nuchal region of the occipital bone are indicators of the male sex. In contrast, female skulls

Table 2   Sexual Characteristics of the Pelvis

Trait	Male	Female
Symphysis	High, narrow	Low, wide
Subpubic angle	V-shaped	U-shaped, round
Obturator foramen	Large, ovoid	Triangular
Sciatic notch	Narrow, deep	Wide, 70-90 degrees
Sacroiliac articulation	Large, straight	Small, oblique
Ilium	High, vertical	Wide
Sacrum	Long, narrow, straight	Short, broad, curved
Pelvic inlet	Heart-shaped	Circular, elliptical
Acetabulum	Large	Small

Modified from Krogman, M. M., *The Human Skeleton in Forensic Medicine*, second edition, Charles C Thomas, Springfield, IL, 1973, pp. 129, 155, 190. With permission.

are more gracile, meaning they do not present the heavy bony development of male skulls. As mentioned earlier, the mandible also represents sexual differences. Males tend to have broad "squarish" chins while females have more "V-shaped" chins (Figure 38). Although the common wisdom is that the skull is the most important feature of the skeleton, using it alone to determine sex is much less accurate than using only the pelvis. Again, the best technique is to use all the available bones (Table 3).

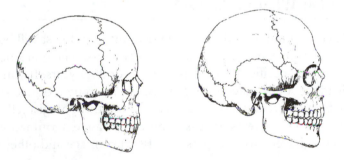

Figure 38   The skull on the left has a smoother, more rounded vault and a smaller chin; it is female. The more rugged skull on the right has male characteristics. (Drawings courtesy of L. Schulzkump. M.D.)

Long bones also differ between males and females; however, the differences are subtle and are identified primarily through measurements and statistical analysis. Both the length and diameter of the bones are measured and when compared to charts derived from many skeletal measurements, can give an indication of sex. Experience is the only way to learn to accurately make those measurements. The diameter of the heads of the humerus and the femur have been shown to be very useful. Unfortunately, these parts of the skeleton are delicate and are often damaged if not properly handled.

Table 3   Sexual Characteristics of the Skull

Trait	Male	Female
Supraorbital ridge (ridge above the eyes)	Robust	Gracile
Occipital protuberance (base of skull)	Robust	Gracile
Mastoid processes (bony process behind ear canal)	Long, broad	Short
Chin	U-shaped, square	V-shaped

Modified from Krogman, M. M., *The Human Skeleton in Forensic Medicine,* second edition, Charles C Thomas, Springfield, IL, 1973, pp. 129, 155, 190. With permission.

Unfortunately, the pelvis and skull are not present in every forensic case. If these bones are not available the determination of sex is going to be tentative, not definite. In such cases, the forensic anthropologist will use as many techniques as necessary to make the determination. In some cases, DNA testing for sex may be appropriate. However, if there are no clear results, it is better to acknowledge that rather than to force the skeleton into one sex or the other, as forcing the determination may cause an error.

Question #8: What is the age?

The age determination provided by a physical anthropologist will be a range, for example, 2½–3 years, 15–17 years, or 50+ years. There are no skeletal clues that allow a specific age such as 12 years or 25½ years. If you get such a determination, you should be suspicious. Trying to be too precise is likely to result in being inaccurate. For example, if the anthropologist tells you that the age range is 17–19 years, that is a more accurate determination than if the anthropologist tells you the person is 18 years of age and other possibilities are ignored.

Determining age partially depends on the general age of the skeleton. The younger the individual, the narrower the age range; the older the person the wider the range. The reason for this sliding range is simple. When very young, there are many biological changes going on in the soft tissue and bones of the body that occur at fairly regular times and rates. As a person reaches biological maturity, the number and rate of developmental changes goes down and the body is in a maintenance mode. As one enters the 40s, 50s, and older, regular changes are less common but degenerative changes can occur. While some of these are regular, many are related to the person's own life history.

Age determination is most accurate for infants and children. Under three, age can be given in a 3- to 4-month range. For children 3–15 years of age, the range increases to 6–18 months. Between about 15 and 25 years, the range may be 1–3 years. After about 35–40 years, age estimates may be given in 5–10 year spans.

One of the keys to differentiation between the skeletons of children and adults is the presence of epiphyses. Epiphyses are growth centers that occur in all bones but are most evident on long bones. These epiphyses are separated from the shafts of the bones by an epiphyseal plate made of cartilage. During decomposition of the body, cartilage is lost and the epiphyses may separate from the shafts of the bones. If the shafts have no bone ends attached then you are looking at a child's skeleton. Because these epiphyses fuse to the shafts of different bones at rather specific ages, the areas of fusion help to pinpoint a child's age. It is necessary to identify the sex of a child's skeleton when estimating age because a girl's epiphyses close at an earlier age. Identifying these changes is one more reason why it is essential to have a forensic anthropologist involved. It is probable that no one else will be able to make this age determination (Figure 39).

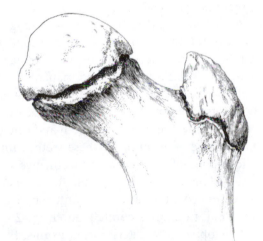

Figure 39   This drawing shows the femur at the stage at which the epiphysis for the head and greater trochanter are not fused. (Drawing courtesy of L. Schulz-kump, M.D.)

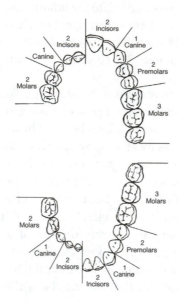

Figure 40 Deciduous (left side) and permanent (right side) teeth differ in size and shape. Care must be taken to recover all portions of the dentition in order to assure accurate aging. (Drawing courtesy of L. Schulzkump, M.D.)

Dental development is another important determinant of age, but that task also requires specific training. Particularly in the young, teeth give some of the best age indicators, but they also can be difficult to identify. Up to the age of about 6, children have only deciduous teeth. From age 6–13 there will be varying combinations of deciduous and permanent teeth. After age 13 only permanent teeth are found but not all are immediately present. The third molar usually erupts at about age 17 (Figure 40). X-rays of the maxilla and mandible in children show the unerupted teeth and can give an accurate age determination. The time of eruption of these teeth, combined with the completion of root formation of the permanent teeth, give a good indication of age up to about 25. Many charts are available for determining age from teeth (Table 4). You will need either a forensic anthropologist or an odontologist to interpret dental findings accurately. After age 25, developmental changes have virtually stopped and deterioration begins. Evidence of wear, deterioration, and type and style of dental restoration may be used as gross indicators of age.

The skull can be helpful in determining age as well. The sutures in the vault of the skull are the areas where the separate bones are joined. In infancy the sutures are wide open and large fontanels are present on the top of the skull. The posterior fontanel closes by the end of the first year and the anterior fontanel is closed by the end of the second year. The other sutures are less

Table 4   Growth Chronology in Human Dentition

Tooth	Eruption	Root Completed
Deciduous Dentition		
Maxillary teeth		
Incisor 1	7.5 months	1.5 years
Incisor 2	9 months	2.0 years
Canine	18 months	3.25 years
Milk 1	14 months	2.5 years
Milk 2	24 months	3.0 years
Mandibular teeth		
Incisor 1	6 months	1.5 years
Incisor 2	7 months	1.5 years
Canine	16 months	3.25 years
Milk 1	12 months	2.25 years
Milk 2	20 months	3.0 years
Permanent Dentition		
Maxillary teeth		
Incisor 1	7–8 years	10 years
Incisor 2	8–9 years	11 years
Canine	11–12 years	13–15 years
Premolar 1	10–11 years	12–13 years
Premolar 2	11–12 years	12–14 years
Molar 1	6–7 years	9–10 years
Molar 2	12–13 years	14–16 years
Molar 3	17–21 years	18–25 years
Mandibular teeth		
Incisor 1	6–7 years	9 years
Incisor 2	7–8 years	10 years
Canine	9–10 years	12–14 years
Premolar 1	10–12 years	12–13 years
Premolar 2	11–12 years	13–14 years
Molar 1	6–7 years	9–10 years
Molar 2	11–13 years	14–15 years
Molar 3	17–21 years	18–25 years

Modified from Wuehrmann, A.H., and Manson-Hing, L.R., *Dental Radiology,* second edition, C.V. Mosby, St. Louis, MO, 1969, p. 258. With permission.

well defined but ten sutures ectocranially (outside surface) and endocranially (inside skull surface) can be identified. Although the regularity of suture closure differs between endo- and ectocranial sutures, they are still useful. These will close or fuse in a relatively consistent pattern and this pattern can give an age range. The problem is that this range is quite broad and provides only an estimate rather than a definite age (Figure 41).

The pubic symphysis which is the surface of each of the pubic bones that meets in front (Figure 42) also can be used to estimate age and is most

Figure 41   The ectocranial sutures are easily seen, however, they provide only a broad age estimate. (Photo courtesy of R.B. Pickering.)

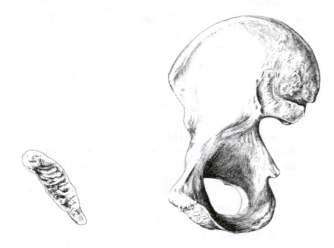

Figure 42   The pubic symphysis is very delicate but it provides one of the best estimates of age on the entire skeleton. (Drawing courtesy of L. Schulzkump, M.D.)

important in adults. The configuration of the face of the symphysis varies with age. A number of charts have been developed that predict age range based on the configuration of the symphysis. Some of the first aging standards were based on medical school cadavers, which tended to emphasize the older ages and consisted of people who may not have been in good health. The need to identify Americans killed in WWII led to a study of the aging changes in the pubic symphysis. Coming from the military context, most of the remains were young (17–25 years) and almost exclusively male. In recent decades, new studies have focused on symphyseal age changes in females. A complicating factor in using these changes in females is that childbirth causes irregular wear and tear on the pubic surface. There are two implications here: first, it is inappropriate to use the male standards to determine the age of the female symphysis, and vice versa and second, the irregularity of change resulting from giving birth (or not having given birth) creates more variable changes on the symphysis and therefore, makes accurate age estimation more difficult. This technique requires a great deal of experience because the changes are subtle.

Two other areas of the body deserve special mention when discussing epiphyseal fusion. The appearance and fusion of epiphyses on the iliac crest of the pelvis and medial end of the clavicle are used to produce an age estimate for the age range between 18 and 35. The difficulty is that the epiphyses, like all such portions, are relatively small, yet they occur on what generally looks like an adult skeleton. It is important that the clavicles and pelvis be examined in the field to see if the epiphyses are there. If they are present but not fused, special care should be taken to collect and label them.

A final age indicator is the amount of arthritic change found on the skeleton. Unlike epiphyseal fusion and the other indicators discussed so far, arthritis is a degenerative change that is specific to the individual. The changes can be affected by variations such as sex, weight, occupation, diet, activities, injuries, and culture. Rates of degenerative change will not necessarily be consistent. Therefore, these changes should only be used as a general indicator of age. For example, no degenerative change probably indicates a young adult. Severe arthritic lipping probably, but not always, indicates an older adult. Changes on the vertebrae are more reliable than changes on the long bones, but all are relative, (Figure 43).

To determine age it is necessary to look at the teeth, the skull, the vertebrae, the pelvis, and the long bones and make your estimate based on all the indicators you find. And it will be an estimate as you need more information than just skeletal remains to be exact.

Question #9: What is the stature?

An experienced physical anthropologist can estimate the height of an individual if complete long bones are present. This is done by accurately measuring the long bones and comparing these measurements to charts based on regression formulae that have been developed after many measurements

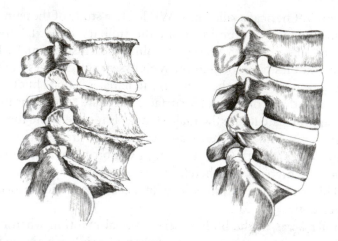

Figure 43 The section of spine on the left shows bony lipping and a slight flattening associated with spinal arthritis. The segment on the right represents the lower spine of a young healthy adult. (Drawings courtesy of L. Schulzkump, M.D.)

of skeletal remains (Figure 44). Long bones of the legs provide a more accurate estimate of height than long bones of the arms. It is necessary to know both the race and sex of the skeleton when using the charts because the charts differ for the sexes within each racial category. To some extent you also need to know the age of the person since we all begin to lose some height in our 50s when our intervertebral disks begin to degenerate. Even after accurately doing these measurements the figure for the height will be an estimate and can only be given as a range. The charts give a mean height from long bone measurements; your individual could be an inch taller or shorter than that mean. If your "expert" gives a specific height, be suspicious. A range is the only thing that can be accurately determined because each formula has its own error range.

Although more difficult to analyze and less accurate, broken long bones or specific portions of long bones also can be used to estimate height. There are charts for estimating long bone lengths from fragments of bones. The chance of error in determining stature from partial remains is even greater because you are basing an estimate of stature on an estimate of long bone length. While not the best situation, you may have to use this technique, particularly in cases where bodies have been severely traumatized.

It borders on the impossible to determine an individual's weight from skeletal remains. Weight fluctuates throughout life. It also looks different on different people. For example, two people may have the same weight, but if one is athletic and muscular while the other is sedentary and over-fat, they will carry their weight differently and may not be perceived in the same way.

Figure 44 Measuring long bones such as this femur allows the anthropologist to estimate the height of an individual. (Photo courtesy of Rick Wicker/DMNH.)

Some experts will give a weight range based on height, sex, and robusticity of muscle attachments. If they apply the WAG (wild-assed guess!) principle they can come up with a possible weight.

Question #10: What are the individual characteristics of the remains?

After all this analysis, what do you know? You have estimates of the class characteristics concerning sex, age, race, and stature which place your subject in a specific group, but you still have not answered the question of who this person is.

You need more information to specifically identify a person. You need to determine if there are any special characteristics that can help identify the remains further. Dental changes including teeth missing before death and

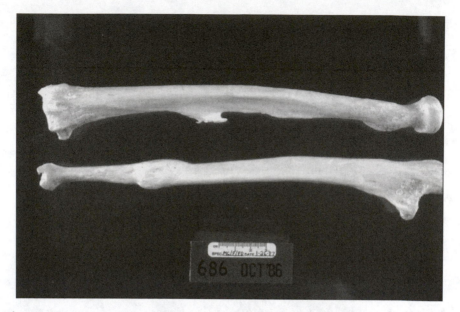

Figure 45   This person suffered from a fracture of both bones of the forearm. Although it healed, deformity from the fracture is clearly visible. (Photo courtesy of R.B. Pickering.)

dental reconstructions are different in each person. Dental X-rays that match your subject give an identification. Skeletal changes including evidence of fractures during life, reconstruction of the skeleton including surgical implants such as screws, plates, and prostheses, and congenital anomalies can lead to almost certain identification (Figures 45 and 46). Arthritic changes that can be compared on X-rays taken during the subject's life with X-rays of the skeletal remains also can make identification probable. Arthritic changes in the spine are more accurate than changes in the joints of the extremities.

Any pathologic changes on the remains may aid the identification process. Take, as an example, the case of a man who detonated a case of dynamite under his car. He had told friends that he was planning to be picked up by a spaceship. They got most of him, but the parts of his car and remains that were found were scattered over several hundred yards of mountain cliff and canyon. The recovery team was able to find a license plate that identified the car and the owner, but the body was so incomplete and mangled that visual identification was impossible. The team did find most of his calvarium which provided eye and hair color. His maxilla was edentulous and no dental plate was found so dental identification was not possible. One critical part, his left hand, was found. The middle and distal phalanges of his left index, middle, and ring fingers had been surgically amputated. Driver's license records provided

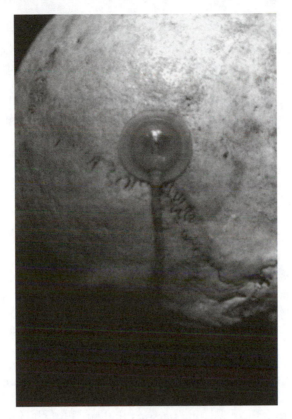

Figure 46   A cranial shunt is an example of a surgically implanted appliance that provides a clue to the person's medical history. (Photo courtesy of D.H. Ubelaker.)

information that the owner of the destroyed car had identical hair and eye color as our subject. Hospital records of the suspected subject confirmed that he had identical finger amputations. Our identification was complete.

Certain kinds of illnesses that occur during life leave marks on bones that can give hints for identification. Bone infections, tuberculosis, rickets, scurvy, and some other diseases will leave permanent bony deformities that are different in each individual. Most of the people who have suffered from these diseases will have X-ray records in hospitals and physicians' offices. Comparing after-death X-rays with their medical records can help in identification.

An experienced anthropologist can often identify handedness by examining the bones and muscle attachments in the upper extremities. The length and circumference of the long bones of the dominant arm tend to be slightly larger than those in the other arm. While this does not give specific identification, it does give you one more piece of evidence in your investigation.

Summary

If you are the investigator who gets the call from someone who thinks he has just discovered some human bones, structure your recovery and investigation to answer these ten questions in sequence. It is the only way to ensure that your investigation is complete and that you have gained all possible information from these bones. Keep in mind that you will need some expert assistance to answer these questions:

1. Is it bone?
2. Is it human?
3. Is it modern?
4. What bones are present?
5. Is more than one person present?
6. Can cultural affiliation be determined?
7. What is the sex?
8. What is the age?
9. What is the stature?
10. What are the individual characteristics of the remains?

Will the expert who helps you answer these questions identify your subject? No, that is your job. However, this expert is the only one of your team members who can give information that will enable you to narrow your investigation to known missing persons that fit all of the identified characteristics.

Determination of Time Since Death

6

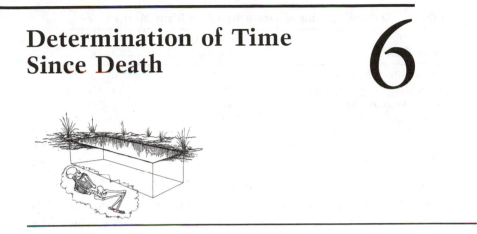

The first question asked whenever a body is discovered is, "Who was this person?" The second question is, "When did this person die?" It makes no difference if it is a fresh body or skeletal remains; you still need to know the answers to those questions. In forensic cases that answer may be essential to obtain a conviction. Tying a time of death to a known victim's associates at that time points to possible identification of the perpetrator.

In instances where discovered remains still have flesh present you know that you are dealing with a forensic case and that this is not a body from a historical period. A forensic pathologist's report will help you determine a probable cause and manner of death. In instances where the discovered remains are fully skeletonized the question of whether this is a forensic case may be more difficult to answer. A thorough investigation, including an examination by a forensic anthropologist, will be necessary to make that determination and to identify a possible cause of death. In both circumstances the time of death question still must be answered.

Determining the time of death is almost always difficult. Unless you can find someone who observed the death, the only thing you can say for certain is that your subject died sometime between the time last seen alive and the time the body was found. Without a detailed examination that is all you know. If the body is fresh you can narrow your estimate to a fairly limited range of time. Several post-mortem changes help narrow the suspected range of time since death in recent cases. *Rigor mortis*, the stiffening of voluntary and involuntary muscles, usually starts in the small muscles and stiffens the major muscle groups in 4–8 hours. The entire body and trunk will stiffen in 8–12 hours. The rigor generally endures for 24–48 hours and then the body again becomes flaccid. Several things, especially heat, either external or internal,

Table 5   Estimating Time of Death Based on Rigor Mortis

Observation	Probable Post-Mortem Interval	Range
Warm body — no rigor	0–2 h	0–5 h
Warm body — rigor progressing	2–6 h	1–8 h
Rigor fully established	6–12 h	1–24 h
Rigor disappeared	18–36 h or more	12–48 h or more

From Brady, W. J., *Outline of Death Investigation*, Oregon State Medical Examiners Office, 1982, p. 41.

age, muscle development, and activity of the victim just before death, affect the onset and duration of rigor. Both a hot environment and increased body temperature due to fever or vigorous activity speed the onset of rigor. The onset of rigor is faster in the young and old but slower in heavily muscled individuals. Having said this, however, it is important to emphasize that rigor mortis changes can only give you a range of time since death (Table 5).

Livor mortis, the gravity-produced settling of blood to dependent portions of the body, appears in pressure-free skin surfaces. This produces a color like a bruise. In areas where there is pressure on the body from contact with the ground or some other object or from tight clothing the skin remains blanched and white. This blanching gives useful information about the position of the body at the time of death. Livor mortis appears first as ill-defined blotches that coalesce and become evident in 1–4 hours. Over the next 3–4 hours livor becomes well developed. After an additional 6–12 hours the lividity becomes relatively fixed. Livor should never be used by itself to make a time of death determination; there are too many variables that affect the times of this settling.

Algor mortis, the loss of body heat, begins after death as the body's temperature falls to that of the surrounding environment. This temperature loss is caused by cooling due to convection, radiation, conduction, and evaporation. This loss is highly variable and depends on the body temperature at death, the sex of the body, the type of clothing on the body, how much skin is exposed, and environmental conditions such as temperature, moisture, wind, time of day, and the surface on which the body is lying. With a fresh body you can measure core body temperature with a rectal hypothermia thermometer, but the many variables again limit your prediction of time since death to a WAG. All these changes should be noted on the report done by the coroner or medical examiner, but the best they can give you is a range of time. The range becomes more inaccurate as the time interval since death increases.

If you are dealing with a badly decomposed body or one that is fully skeletonized, your range for estimation is much wider; in fact, determining a time since death can be only an educated guess. An almost infinite number of variables affect the rate of decomposition of a body. These variables can be fitted into two major categories: the body itself and the micro environment in which it was found.

The Body

1. The first consideration is body size. Large bodies take longer to decompose than small bodies.
2. The second important consideration is whether or not the body is intact. Just as in life, an intact skin surface protects a body from assault by noxious organisms. After-death decomposition begins around natural body openings; particularly the head, and then proceeds to areas of the body with the most tissue. If there are wounds on the body there are more openings for organisms ranging from bacteria to insects to carnivores to attack, accelerating decomposition. If the body has been mutilated with parts severed from it, each small part will decompose more rapidly than if it was an intact body.
3. The third consideration is how the body has been handled after death. A nude body lying on the ground will decompose faster than a clothed body. Heavy clothing will slow decomposition more than light clothing. Wrapping a body in plastic or some other similar material will slow the process even more.

A buried body will decompose slowly. Burial in a cast-iron coffin will cause more delay than burial in a pine box, and both will be slower than if the body was buried directly in the ground.

Embalming the body will severely affect the rate of decomposition. In Chapter 4 we mentioned the discovery of residual pink flesh on the bones of Colonel Shy who had been buried 113 years previously. At the time of exhumation his large and small intestines were still morphologically identifiable. His body had been both embalmed and buried in a metal coffin so decomposition was dramatically delayed.

Bones and hair are the last body tissues to disintegrate. President Zachary Taylor, "Old Rough and Ready," died in 1850, 16 months into his presidency. His death was attributed to acute gastroenteritis caused by food poisoning at a midsummer picnic. Due to a persistent rumor that he was poisoned, his body was exhumed for chemical analysis in 1991. At that time, 140 years after death, his hair and bushy eyebrows were still intact although the skin and soft tissue had decomposed. You will be pleased to know that no arsenic was found during this re-examination.

As bones decompose they go through several stages. In the first stage, articular cartilage on the bone ends dries and cracks then disintegrates. In the second stage the bones themselves are "greasy". If bones are found that have a splotchy brown discoloration and a greasy texture it generally means that fat is still present in the bones and that the bones are from a recent death that occurred months, not years ago. In the next stage of decomposition the bones blanch and whiten. Finally, the bone cracks and exfoliates and chips from the surface flake off. Natural post-mortem cracks in teeth have sometimes been mistaken for ante-mortem fractures.

While all this is true, the color and appearance of old bones is not enough to make a specific determination of time since death. These changes can give only a general indication of whether the bones have been exposed to the environment for a long time or a relatively short time. Bones exposed to air and sunlight blanch more quickly. Buried bones may assume the color of the material in which they are buried. In fact, a single bone may show different stains if it is partially exposed and partly buried. In that situation the best stage of bone preservation is the most reliable indicator of time of exposure. The environment itself will affect all of these changes.

The Micro Environment

The variables directly associated with decomposition of the body are relatively straightforward compared to the variables from the micro environment that affect the rate of decomposition.

1. The time of year when the body is exposed dramatically affects decomposition. Cold weather slows the rate while hot weather accelerates it. Frozen bodies don't decompose, as we know from recovered bodies that have been preserved in ice; but bodies that thaw after being frozen for a long time decompose rapidly. At high elevations with frequent temperature extremes, repeated freezing and thawing accelerate decomposition. High humidity also accelerates decomposition.
2. Exposure of the body to direct sunlight hastens decomposition. Shaded areas are cooler and slow down the rate.
3. A buried body will decompose more slowly than one found on the surface, yet acidic soil and high soil moisture content will accelerate decomposition of buried bodies. These were the conditions that existed when Japanese graves were exhumed on Yap Island in 1980. It

was found that skeletal remains buried in late 1944 and early 1945 had almost completely decomposed. The only things found in 12 graves were tooth crowns and a few long bone slivers. The opposite occurred in Western Illinois where a 7000-year-old neonatal skeleton that had been buried in dry, non-acidic soil was exhumed in good condition. A body submerged in water will decompose more slowly than if exposed on the ground surface, unless it is attacked by sharks, fish, or crustaceans. The FBI pulled a virtually intact body from a northern lake where it had been submerged for 30 years in water at a temperature of 36–38°F.

4. Plant growth can sometimes give a hint as to how long a body has been exposed. Plants go through a defined cycle, and if plants have grown around or through a skeleton that cycle length indicates how long that body has been there. Plants also can accelerate deterioration of the body.

5. Animal and bird scavengers can have a dramatic effect on the appearance of a body. Large scavengers tend to devour a corpse in a characteristic sequence beginning with the torso and viscera. They may drag parts of the body to secluded areas for feeding; disarticulated remains may be found 100 m or more away from the original body location and even in dens or burrows. State wildlife officials may be needed to help you locate dens. These scavengers are usually nocturnal, feeding at night, especially in winter. Smaller scavengers, such as rodents, feed at the site and usually only on well-skeletonized remains; consumption of the bones gives them a source of dietary minerals. These rodents leave characteristic tooth marks on bones. It would be unusual to find bones exposed for a year or more that did not have such marks.

6. Nothing affects the rate of body decomposition more than insects. This is a place where bringing in another team member, an entomologist, can be invaluable. Insect activity varies from yard to yard, state to state, region to region, and season to season. Only an expert can provide that kind of information and he will need to be at the scene to collect specimens in order to provide a full story.

Necrophilous (dead-flesh eating) insects arrive at an exposed body quickly and different species arrive in a relatively predictable sequence. Blow flies can show up in minutes. Flies lay eggs which hatch into larvae. Fly larvae, which can live in a semi-liquid medium, are the first insects attracted to a decomposing remains and the first to colonize one. These fly larvae (maggots) are responsible for the rapid decomposition of a corpse's tissue. Maggots grow rapidly and pass through three stages. After reaching the third stage the larvae crawl away from the corpse and burrow into the soil to find a safe place to enter their next life stage, the pupa. Later, as the corpse is drying, beetles and other insects move in to complete the job.

Different phases of insect development on, under, and around the corpse are evidence of how long the body has been exposed. The insect's life cycle depends on time and temperature but can be affected by relative humidity, daylight hours, and moisture. Insects are cold-blooded and, for each species, there is generally a threshold temperature below which no development takes place.

The entomologist will collect insect specimens in all developmental phases from on, under, and around the corpse as well as any that might be found at autopsy. If possible, live samples also should be collected and kept alive. If reared until they reach adult form they will be more easily and accurately identifiable, giving the entomologist an opportunity to observe their behavior. Immature phases can be reared in an artificial environment that mimics what was present where the body was found. The time interval for maturation may give an indication of the time that elapsed while the body was exposed. Collected adult specimens are kept alive so they can be observed for habits and normal life span.

An experienced forensic entomologist can use this information to estimate the duration of the post-mortem interval or time since death. This interval will be given in a range with a maximum and minimum limit. The maximum limit is determined by the species of insects present and the weather "windows" available for activity of these species. This information can yield an estimate of the earliest time the body could have been exposed to insect activity. The minimum limit is estimated from the age of developing immature insects collected at the time of body discovery.

If you accumulate all of this scientific information you sometimes can narrow your estimation of time since death to a fairly limited range, but unless someone witnessed the death, do not offer anything other than a range of time. Reporting a specific date and time without definite evidence moves your report into the realm of guesswork and calls your credibility into question.

Remember, guesswork does not stand up in court.

Eight Essential Environmental Categories of Information

If you are going to estimate the time since death for a decomposing body, there are certain categories of information that you must acquire if your estimate is to have any scientific validity and acceptability as evidence in court:

1. Season of year with hours of daylight and darkness
2. Temperature ranges, both daytime highs and nighttime lows for entire period
3. Humidity ranges for the entire period
4. Clouds, precipitation, snow cover
5. pH of soil for buried bodies
6. Plant growth around body
7. Scavengers common to area and den sites
8. Insects common to area at each season.

Special Techniques — Their Value and Limitations

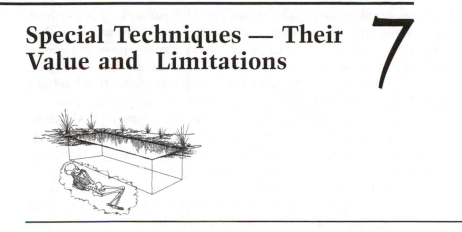

The fact that new innovations are being made in all fields of science every day isn't news, rather, it is a trend that continues to pick up speed and complexity. Keeping up with the flow of information in any single field is difficult for most people. Forensic investigation is an eclectic field that borrows techniques and procedures from many fields, thereby increasing the information burden dramatically. As each new promising technique becomes available, it seems to provide answers to old questions and promises to make our work easier. Yet, each new technique needs to be evaluated and understood so that it may be applied properly. For example, a carpenter would never use a circular saw to cut metal pipe and a surgeon does not use a desk stapler to sew up a patient. Each tool and technique has its proper use as well as its improper ones. Being able to tell the difference is what separates the professional from the amateur. So it is in forensic investigation. There are more techniques and specialists available today than ever before and that very abundance offers a challenge.

This section discusses some of the innovations in forensic analysis and provides some suggestions about when they can and cannot be used properly.

Facial Reconstruction

Leading story on the 6 o'clock news — "A skeleton was recently found in a field near town. The skull and jaw were found intact. The coroner says no one locally is missing so the decision has been made to do a facial reconstruction to see what the person looked like. A local archaeologist and part-time art teacher have volunteered to do the reconstruction. Authorities are confident that they will soon identify the deceased."

Does this anecdote sound silly or familiar? Unfortunately, it is a little of both. For reasons that have nothing to do with science, this technique has become popular in recent years after being used in mystery shows and books. Courses in facial reconstruction have been offered around the country by people of varying experience and knowledge. Facial reconstruction has been touted as the best hope of finding a quick answer to the identification of a skeletal remains. It is certainly true that at various times facial reconstruction has led to the identification of a remains or to the capture of a perpetrator; however, if the history and assumptions of facial reconstruction are examined, confidence in this technique may ebb considerably.

Facial reconstruction is a broad term used to describe a number of methods that have a common goal — trying to determine if a skull can be matched to a particular face. The concept sounds reasonable. A face gets much of its form from the underlying support of the skull. If one could somehow show that the form of the skull and the face, not to mention the shape and position of the teeth, were identical to a missing person then the identity of the skull could be determined.

Facial reconstruction is a mixture of art and science. The science provides the measurements and the understanding of the relationship between the face and underlying skull. Through sculptural art, the scientific data is transformed into a life-like face that is recognizable as a real human face that has meaning to the viewer. For many years, museums have used facial reconstructions to show visitors how ancient people and our pre-human ancestors looked. The famous fossil skull of Lucy, our 2.2-million-year-old ancestor, the Ice Man, and many other dry bones from the distant past have been brought to life through facial reconstruction. The results are educational, appealing, and haunting, but they are not forensic (Figure 47). In these cases the museum and artist are trying to convey a picture of life long ago, not trying to identify an individual and have their results stand up in court.

Although simple in concept, making direct facial reconstructions is more complicated than might be thought. Finding a way to do it consistently and accurately has eluded scientists for nearly a century. Different techniques have been tried, each one reflecting the state of thinking and technology of the time. Although facial reconstruction has some potential value, it also is fraught with dangerous pitfalls. This section discusses some of the major techniques that have been used and some of the problems that exist.

Direct Facial Reconstruction

Perhaps the oldest type of direct facial reconstruction involves the building of a face with clay or wax over the actual skull or a cast of the skull. Many

Figure 47 Facial reconstruction of the 4000-year-old Ice Man. Facial reconstructions in museum exhibits can be very realistic and are very effective in creating a personality, but their use in forensic cases may be helpful or misleading. (Photo courtesy of J. Gurche.)

anatomists and physical anthropologists of the 19th and early 20th century have tried to describe and quantify the variability they saw in the human body. They were often interested in differences attributed to sex and race. During this period, the new science of statistics was being used to systematize and standardize visual observations. These trends toward quantification and statistical interpretation converged in an early attempt to reconstruct faces on skulls (Figure 48). These scientists recognized that they needed to identify important points on the skull that give the face its shape. They also had to determine the thickness of soft tissues including skin, muscle, and fat over various parts of the skull. Recognizing that there were differences in tissue thicknesses between men and women, and theorizing that there might be differences between races, earlier scientists used medical school cadavers to gather data on tissue thicknesses in the various sex and race groups, e.g., white males and females and black males and females.

Defining landmarks on the skull for measurement was a subject of great interest, hard work, and much debate. The result was the identification and definition of many of the measuring points that are still in use today. Learning how to measure a skull properly is one of the arcane but necessary skills that all forensic anthropologists still must learn. The difficulty is that skulls are,

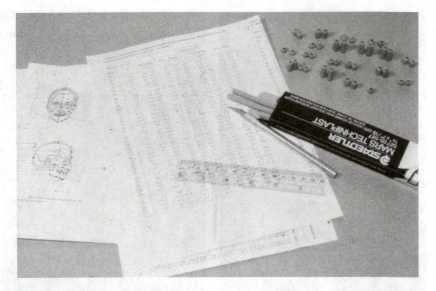

Figure 48 Average thicknesses of skin, fat, and muscle over many standard anthropometric points of the skull are the basis for facial reconstruction. (Photo courtesy of R. Evenhouse.)

in fact, quite variable, much more than most people think. Finding the exact measuring point sometimes can be difficult (Figure 49). Once found, measuring the points precisely can be difficult. Errors of more than 3 or 4 mm are unacceptable for most measurements. However, assuming that the measurements are properly taken, there is still the problem of what they mean. As mentioned earlier, tissue thicknesses are based on research using cadavers. Obviously, one important problem is the extent to which one can assume that measurements taken on dead bodies are the same as those in living persons. The body is always in a state of change, before death and after; therefore, the extent to which death has changed tissue thicknesses to the point of statistical significance is debatable. The second concern is that while the cranial landmarks are all the same, individuals are different. Statistically creating an average has some value for describing populations or other groups, but it may not provide accurate information on how much fat and muscle and skin is over a particular point in the skull of a specific person. As if these concerns were not enough, there is the knotty problem of the samples themselves. Scientists today know we should not assume that a group of medical school cadavers are representative of the population as a whole. At the time these studies were done, most of the cadavers were indigents. Their diet, health, and other characteristics did not represent the population at large. Therefore, if the sample is not representative, the data derived from such a sample cannot be truly representative. The final concern is that medical

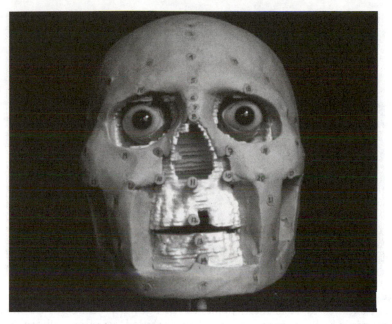

Figure 49   A partial reconstruction of an ancient Egyptian skull shows the anthropometric points that define tissue thicknesses. To move from this point to a recognizable face takes artistic skill as well as scientific knowledge. (Photo courtesy of R. Evenhouse.)

and anthropological studies have demonstrated that the American population today is not biologically the same as the American population of 100 years ago. We tend to be taller, heavier, and better nourished; some might say overnourished. Therefore, it is quite likely that old data do not adequately describe our population today.

With all of these problems, the question might be, "Why are we still using this technique?" There are a number of answers to this question. First, the concept is still a potentially useful one, but the data need to be revised. To that end, a new database comprised of modern cases is being developed at the University of Tennessee. Anthropologists from all over the U.S. send cranial measurements and other biological data from their forensic cases to the University of Tennessee to be added to the database (Figure 50). Not only is this information more contemporary, it may be more representative of the American population than the older cadaver data.

New medical imaging techniques also are being used to solve some of the old problems. Every day thousands of people undergo CAT scan, MRI, or other sophisticated imaging procedure in hospitals and medical laboratories. The results are high-resolution images of the patient in life, not death. Measurements of tissue from these living patients are preferable to those from

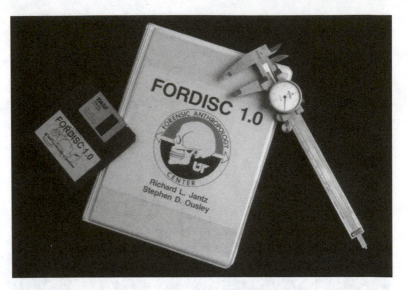

Figure 50 FORDISC is a software program that compares the measurements from one skull to those of many populations. The statistical comparison can aid in determining the sex and race of unidentified remains. (Photo by Rick Wicker/DMNH)

cadavers. The challenge has always been how to compare dry bone-skulls with living human heads. Fortunately, medical imaging technology is now able to show both hard and soft tissues in such a way that comparison with dry skulls may be possible. A team at the Center for Human Simulation at the University of Colorado Health Sciences Center under the direction of Dr. Victor Spitzer and anthropologist Amy Schilling is working on a project that will try to use some of the most modern medical imaging equipment to consistently and accurately measure soft tissue at specified landmarks on the skull. If this project is successful, facial reconstruction may be conducted on a more reliable database.

Craniaofacial Superimposition

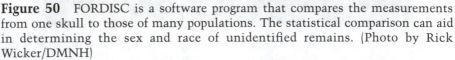

Photographic superimposition in its simplest form includes creating a photographic image of the skull that can be superimposed on an ante-mortem photo of the person. Superimposition assumes that photographs accurately reflect the details of the face. While using a camera solves some of the problems of direct cranial reconstruction, such as tissue thickness or the ability of the artist, new problems are created. One of the most critical is how to photograph the skull in the exact position and at the same distance as the ante-mortem photo. Within craniofacial superimposition, a number of different techniques have been proposed by investigators not only in the U.S. and Canada but also in Europe, China, and Australia.

One of the most famous examples of early attempts at craniofacial superimposition was the Buck Ruxton case in Scotland. Dr. Ruxton had done away with both his wife and female housekeeper. Because of his medical background, he knew that various parts of the body, such as fingerprints and ears, could be used to identify the body and thereby lead to the killer. Therefore, he dismembered both victims and further dissected soft tissue from bone. He then packaged the remains and deposited them in parcels across the landscape. As more bundles were found, the difficulty of identification superseded shock over this grisly case.

It became clear that two women had been the victims and that they were roughly the same age. Eventually, suspicion did focus on Dr. Ruxton whose wife and housekeeper were mysteriously missing. Yet, there was no way to identify the dismembered remains as these two women.

With good ante-mortem photos of each victim available, John Glaister, Professor of Forensic Medicine at the University of Glasgow, decided to try to identify both women through photo superimposition. One of the principal difficulties in this technique is placing the skull at the same distance and in the position as the head in the picture. Fortunately for the case, Mrs. Ruxton had been photographed shortly before her death. The local town photographer was able to reconstruct the distances and angles in the antemortem photo by using the same gown and tiara in the post-mortem photo. The match between ante- and post-mortem photos along with other evidence was good enough to identify Mrs. Ruxton and to convict Dr. Ruxton.

In more recent times, others have experimented with this technique. One of the most notable techniques was developed by Tadao Furue, forensic anthropologist at the U.S. Army CIL, first in Japan and then in Hawaii. Furue used a system which included a large format camera, front surface mirror, and a beam splitter or partial mirror to create his superimpositions. This technique allowed him to use an original life photo to position the skull correctly. In this way, a transparency photo of the skull could be laid over the life photo to see if they matched. Klonaris and Furue used a variation of this technique to match a fragment of maxilla without teeth with an ante-mortem dental X-ray. In fact, forensic odontologists probably use this technique more than other specialists, because dental X-rays are commonly taken and the structure and position of teeth, the surrounding bone of the jaws, and odontological repairs provide a great variety of structure which can be compared between ante- and post-mortem images.

Video Superimposition

The introduction of video cameras and computers has taken photo super-imposition a step further. Instead of using mirrors and still cameras, two video cameras are used: one focuses on the skull, while the other image is centered on the ante-mortem photo. As with still photos, the ante-mortem image is used to orient the skull. The difference is that a video mixer is used to superimpose the two images through the cameras.

Regardless of the specific techniques of facial reconstruction or cranio-facial superimposition, the question remains, "How similar do the skull and photo have to be in order to match?" Most researchers agree that craniofacial superimposition is a good technique for excluding potential matches. If the ante- and post-mortem images do not fit, they probably represent two different people. However, is the technique so accurate that if two images match, they represent one and only one person? Unfortunately, a detailed evaluation and test of the various techniques has not been done systematically, so this question remains unanswered.

There are cases in which each of these techniques has been used successfully, yet, both can be misleading. Virtually all the investigators who have proposed one of these techniques say that it should never be used by itself to establish identity; other evidence is always required. The authors of this book cannot improve on that recommendation. Facial reconstruction or craniofacial superimposition may prove to be useful, but it should not be relied upon by itself to determine identity.

Footprint Impression Analysis

For more than a decade, the study of footprints and shoe prints has been associated with the name of Louise M. Robbins. Depending on your perspective, she was either a great scientist who added a powerful weapon to the forensic arsenal or she was a charlatan and a hired gun. In either case, she conducted a great deal of research on impressions left by bare and shod feet while causing considerable controversy along the way.

There is no question that feet and the shoes that cover them have many important identifying traits. There are both normal and abnormal differences in foot size and shape and old injuries can affect the way people walk. The type of shoes also can affect foot shape. Podiatrists are well aware of the damage that pointed-toed, high-heeled "fashion" shoes have caused to women's feet. Similarly, tight, pointed-toed, cowboy boots also change the natural shape of feet.

If a foot or shoe print is made in a soft material such as wet sand, mud, paint, or blood, it may provide clues to who made the print. However, in forensic situations, prints are rarely clear, complete, or easy to read. A great deal of research is needed to understand the clues of foot and shoe prints. For example, a good shoe print may tell you that the shoe was of a particular brand, style, and size. However, does that description identify the wearer? The following fictional newscast provides an example.

> *Leading story on the 6 o'clock news* — "At a grisly crime scene, police found shoe prints in the blood of the victim. Investigators say that they probably belong to the killer and were made as he fled the scene. The shoes have been identified as Nike running shoes, size 10. Police are now searching for the killer."

Assuming that the description of the brand and other details are correct, the investigator still has a huge task ahead. The shoe print was made by one shoe out of millions. The investigator must find characteristics of that print that separate the one shoe from all others of its type and size. The additional question for the investigator is "Whose foot was in the shoe?" While it is clear that a person's footprint may be unique, does that mean that the shoe print of that foot is unique? There is considerable disagreement on this point.

The best advice regarding foot and shoe prints is that they need to be recorded as accurately as possible. Clear, close-up photos with good lighting and a length scale are essential. Photos from different positions are important, as well.

Osteon Counting

Osteon counting (*an osteon is the microscopic bone unit of compact bone, consisting of the haversian canal and surrounding lamellae*) is a specialized technique for determining the age of a person. While a person is alive, the bones are alive as are the soft tissue organs of the body. Bone is made of specialized cells that grow, die, and are replaced. More than 20 years ago, anthropologists discovered that looking at the ratio of different types of bone cells under the microscope might be useful in determining age (Figure 51). Research has continued into the microscopic changes that occur in bone. Osteon counting continues to be a useful tool in determining age, particularly in adults where other gross developmental changes have ceased. Osteon counting requires special equipment and training to take and read the samples. The forensic anthropologist is the best person to determine if this technique is appropriate or not.

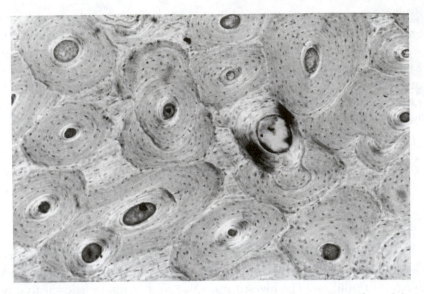

Figure 51   Osteons are bone cells that develop and change throughout life. The osteon counting technique requires specialized training and equipment. It can be very useful if the remains is incomplete and lacks many of the bones used in other methods of age determination. (Photo courtesy of S. Stout.)

Bitemark Analysis

Teeth have many characteristics that can be important in forensic cases, particularly in the identification of remains, skeletal or complete. The number and shape of the teeth, as well as their position, modification by dentists, and evidence of disease all provide useful individuating traits.

Over the past 20 years, the study of the impressions of teeth left on bite victims has become a valuable forensic tool. The concept is simple: a bitemark should be characteristic of the teeth that made it. If a bitemark can be recorded through photography or as an impression, then it can be compared to an impression made by a potential assailant. Logically, the more unusual the dentition, the more significant the bitemark becomes in identification.

Bitemarks can be left in virtually any medium that is soft enough to bite yet stable enough to retain its shape. There are cases in which burglars have bitten into apples, cheese, or other foods which were then left at the crime scene. If recovered and preserved, such items can provide valuable evidence. Bitemarks often have been found on the victims of sexual assault and child abuse and have been used to convict the perpetrators.

Bitemark analysis has become a sophisticated specialty, particularly within the odontology community. If such marks are found on a remains or some other material, the medicolegal officer should contact a forensic odontologist as soon as possible to see how to preserve and record the mark.

ABO Blood Typing

Determining the ABO blood group from a sample of fresh blood or from a dried stain is a common procedure. Along with other evidence, blood stain analysis may be used to place a person at a crime scene, or possibly to completely exclude that person. To a large extent DNA extraction technology has superseded the reliance on the ABO blood system for identification. Normally, this kind of testing is totally within the purview of the crime scene laboratory.

A variation of blood testing, however, is related to forensic anthropology. Called the absorption-elution technique, these ABO blood group determinations have been conducted on samples of hair, bone, and fingernail with some success. Dr. Shoichi Yada has used this technique on forensic cases and archaeological remains. His work has demonstrated that even dry bone and small amounts of hair can yield ABO information. In the mid-1970s, Pickering and others tested the absorption-elution technique and applied it to American remains from Southeast Asia with some success. The results showed that even hair as short as 2 cm could be used successfully (Figure 52).

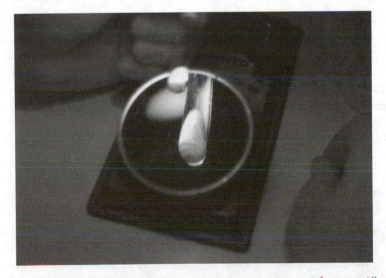

Figure 52 Small hair samples show a positive reaction with a specific blood antigen.

Forensic toxicologists also can determine blood type from skeletal remains. Determining blood type is useful as a means of eliminating a large number of persons. If the skeletal remains are discovered to be from an individual with type O blood, then all people with type A, B, or AB blood are eliminated. However, blood typing, or paleoserology, sometimes yields false-positive or false-negative results, so it should not be relied on as the sole indicator of identification. For instance, certain plants can cause false-positive results on remains that have been buried in the ground. Therefore, in addition to testing the human sample, it is necessary to also know about the plants in the immediate vicinity of the remains and possibly do an ABO test on the soil.

While this technique is still useful, in light of the rapid development of DNA studies, there are limits on its applicability. It probably should not be used on remains that have been buried in the ground for years unless the body has been protected from the soil. For example, a body in a heavy plastic bag or a coffin might yield accurate results. At the opposite end of the spectrum, a remains that is completely skeletal and has roots growing around and through the bones would not be a good case on which to use the absorption-elution technique. A remains that has decomposed on top of the ground or in a building may also yield reliable ABO results.

Forensic Toxicology

The ability of forensic toxicologists to determine trace amounts of drugs and other toxic elements in skeletal remains has been increased significantly through development of new methods of chemical analysis. Gas chromatograph mass spectrometry is the technique that currently yields the most accurate results. With these instruments, chemists are able to discover small amounts of abnormal chemicals in bone or other tissue and can do so by utilizing small amounts of any tissue.

Several toxic metals can poison human beings, which, if ingested 24–36 hours before death, will leave permanent traces in bones as well as in hair, nails, and skin. The presence of these metals can be found years later. In Chapter 5 we mentioned the search for arsenic in the exhumed body of President Zachary Taylor 141 years after his death. No abnormal amount of arsenic was found, but had it been present, it would have been discovered.

Cadmium, copper, and lead can cause poisoning in humans, but exposure to these metals almost always occurs through industrial poisoning or is accidental. Mercury, which is present in some topical medications and in catalytic agents used in plastic manufacture, and thallium, which is present in insecticides and rodenticides, have been ingested accidentally as well as intentionally in suicides. Arsenic is the most notorious heavy metal. Homicide by arsenic poisoning has been known for years and made famous in the play, *Arsenic and Old Lace.*

Techniques for identification of all of these metals have been known for years and can be done in a variety of ways. The chemical analysis for heavy metals is simpler than for other things that may be important in forensic investigation. More recent developments now allow toxicologists to identify many other chemicals from skeletal remains and to approximate quantification. Joe Levisky, forensic toxicologist for El Paso County, CO, has identified tricyclic antidepressants, over-the-counter cold medications, methamphetamines, amphetamines, benzodiazapines, and heroin through its morphine base. Most have been found in remains less than one year old but could probably be identified in older remains. He has not identified cocaine, but others have found it in skeletal remains. Levisky recommends the femoral head and neck as the best skeletal site for recovery of drugs. The femoral head has a significant blood supply during life and in adults the marrow is about 50% fat; both of which contribute to the ability to recover drugs from bone. Other areas of cancellous bone such as the humeral head, the sternum, and the pelvis should yield similar results if tested.

^{14}C Dating

We talked earlier about ^{14}C dating of bones. Radiocarbon dating, based on the decay of ^{14}C, now permits calculation of the post-mortem interval up to about 45,000 years. Few of us have to worry about prehistoric homicides, so this information is more useful for archaeologists than for death scene investigators.

DNA Testing

The most revolutionary advance in forensic techniques for the positive identification of individuals is based on DNA testing.

DNA is the carrier of the genetic code in humans. It is contained in the genes which occupy a specific location on the chromosomes in the nucleus of each cell. The human genome (the complete set of chromosomes) contains about 3 billion base pairs of DNA. Each person inherits two copies of this genome in 23 pairs of chromosomes, one set from each parent, for a total of 46.

Trying to make sense, or more significant for us, trying to identify an individual from 3 billion base pairs of DNA would seem an impossible task, but it is possible. Recombinant DNA technology allows for the analysis of one DNA fragment at a time, providing an "index" for the human genome and making it possible to locate and isolate individual genes, segments of genes, or nucleotide sequences from the vast DNA library.

Put in its simplest terms, there are several special techniques that make DNA typing possible for forensic identification. Restriction fragment length polymorphism (RFLP) testing, which uses a combination of single locus probes that vary highly among individuals, produces a DNA print or profile. This analysis provides the ability to distinguish the genotype (the genetic constitution of a person) of virtually all individuals except identical twins. Combining that with polymerase chain reaction (PCR) testing yields a powerful tool for forensic analysis, since identification can be made from minuscule samples of semen, blood, hair root, skin, and other tissues including bone marrow.

Just because this testing and identification is possible does not mean that the evidence will be accepted in court without question. Several problems may limit its acceptance. To begin with, the courts are sometimes reluctant to accept new technology. A more important question is the reliability of the evidence. As demonstrated in the "Case of the Century," forensic laboratories have not proven that their testing is foolproof. Labs must perfect techniques that yield consistent, reproducible results and establish controls that make sample mixing impossible before this evidence will be accepted in court with full confidence. Forensic laboratories need an accreditation scheme.

The "Case of the Century" emphasized some points that are even more important for us as death investigators. The chain of evidence must be meticulously documented and maintained so that there can be no question that evidence was contaminated, mixed up, temporarily mislaid, or delayed in getting to the proper testing facility. That is our responsibility and our failure will compromise our case. The moral is: Keep very accurate records.

Skeletal Trauma and Identifying Skeletal Pathology

8

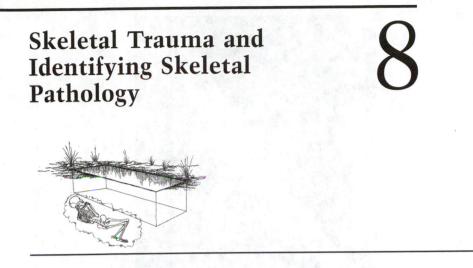

There's a third question that must be answered after "Who is this person and when did this person die?" and that is, "What was the cause of death?" Unfortunately, in many cases you will not learn the cause of death by examining the skeleton. Most of the time, people are killed by injury to the body's major organs. In partially skeletonized or severely traumatized remains, those organs will have decomposed to the point where that evidence has disappeared. Once in a while you get lucky — skeletal trauma is found that gives you clues to the cause of death. The only way to find those clues is to look at the entire skeleton for unusual discontinuities in the bones from some kind of skeletal trauma or some kind of skeletal pathology.

You have to be cautious, though as not all skeletal trauma is related to your subject's demise. There are three distinct times when trauma may occur: ante-mortem, peri-mortem, and post-mortem. If there is evidence of skeletal trauma, the first thing you have to determine is when that trauma occurred. That's often difficult but there may be signs on the bones that help you make that determination.

Ante-Mortem Trauma

Ante-mortem trauma seldom gives any clues to the cause of death, but evidence of it can make identification of your subject possible. Fractures occurring in adults during life, if displaced, almost always heal with some unique residual deformity that is apparent on X-ray (Figure 53). Spinal fractures leave distinctive deformities that also are visible on X-ray and can be

Figure 53   Although properly treated, this femur shows a slight curvature and thickening of the cortex (dense white areas of the shaft) that indicate an earlier fracture. (Photo courtesy of James Quale, M.D., Swedish Medical Center.)

used in identification (Figure 54). Fractures in children usually heal and remodel within a year to the point where no evidence of the fracture remains. However, recent fractures in children are evident for 6–12 months and may aid in identification. Multiple fractures in children and fractures occurring at different ages send up the red flag for child abuse.

A case from Chicago serves as a good example of how old fractures reveal life history. The skeleton of an older man with many healed fractures was found. An examination revealed that the man had old fractures of both forearms, one ankle, and the skull. The fractures appeared to be of about the same age and probably resulted from a severe beating (Figure 55). Once the man was identified, it was discovered that he had led a rough life which involved some mean friends and heavy drinking. He suffered from poor health too. People with poor nutrition do not heal as quickly or as well as those who benefit from a good diet. In addition to the ante-mortem fractures, there was an additional peri-mortem fracture on the skull. The break showed

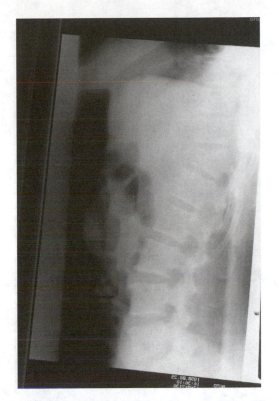

Figure 54   A lateral X-ray of the spine with compression fracture of the T-12 vertebra shows deformity and change in the alignment of the other vertebrae. (Photo courtesy of James Quale, M.D., Swedish Medical Center.)

no signs of healing and was a result of the beating that caused the man's death. Both kinds of fractures were present, but their time of occurrence was critical to the case.

If fractures are treated surgically, the implanted devices such as pins, screws, bolts, nails, or plates will have a distinctive appearance on X-ray. Prostheses used in joint replacements usually are too similar in appearance on X-ray and too common to be distinctive. However, prosthesis designs change and therefore can indicate a range of time when the prosthesis was surgically implanted. Prostheses also are identified by a lot number that will give a time of manufacture, but because the lot size may be several hundred this information may not be helpful (Figure 56). Also be sure to pick up all metal debris at the recovery site as it may be related to your case.

If post-mortem X-rays of a victim are identical to X-rays of a known subject taken during life then it is probable that the victim and the known subject are identical.

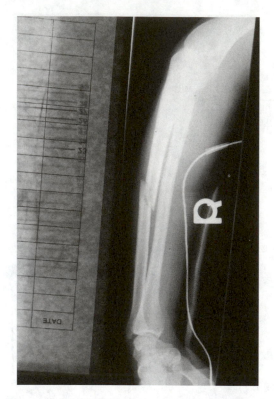

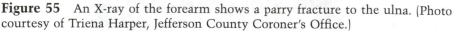

Figure 55 An X-ray of the forearm shows a parry fracture to the ulna. (Photo courtesy of Triena Harper, Jefferson County Coroner's Office.)

Peri-Mortem Trauma

Evidence of peri-mortem trauma can sometimes pinpoint the cause of death. Stab wounds occasionally damage bones, especially ribs. Large knives are often too wide to penetrate the chest without nicking adjacent ribs (Figure 57). The sharp edges of knives will raise a shaving of bone that looks like what you produce when you start whittling on a piece of wood. A hunting knife with a blunt edge may gouge a dent on one rib and cut the adjacent one. Figure 58 shows an unusual case of a stab wound to the side of the skull. The shape is characteristic of the knife's blade. The slight curling of bone rather than a clean break reveals that the wound was made around the time of death and not later.

A gunshot to the head may leave the bullet in the skull as evidence (Figure 59). Even if the bullet is gone, its signature of penetration and fracture will be present. Gunshots to the rest of the skeleton seldom leave a complete bullet as evidence unless it is lodged in a vertebra. Often, however, bullet

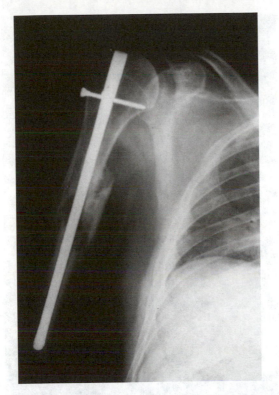

Figure 56   Healing of a severely fractured humerus is aided by an intramedullary rod and screw. Such appliances can be valuable clues in forensic investigations. (Photo courtesy of James Quale, M.D., Swedish Medical Center.)

fragments not apparent to the naked eye will show up on an X-ray (Figure 60). That is one of the reasons that all skeletal remains should be X-rayed.

Peri-mortem blunt trauma to the skull usually produces a depressed fracture with fracture lines radiating out from the point of impact. Figure 61 shows multiple skull fractures caused by massive blunt trauma. A blow to the head of a child often results in separation along suture lines rather than fracture and depression of the bone that was impacted. A blunt instrument such as a hammer or the back of a machete blade may leave a characteristic depression. X-rays are essential to make these determinations.

Dismembered remains may be scattered over a wide area. The perpetrator may have scattered the remains in an attempt to hide them, or scavengers may have carried them off. Unless the victim was killed by an animal, damage to the skeleton caused by animals is most likely the result of post-mortem scavenging. Intentional dismemberment leaves clues that may indicate the type of cutting instrument used, such as a knife, axe, or saw. Figure 62 shows

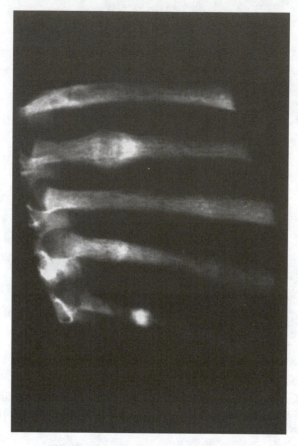

Figure 57   Stab wound to the ribs.

the neck vertebrae from a case in which dismemberment was suspected. After the vertebrae were cleaned and placed in their normal anatomical position, it was clear that the head had been severed and that the blow had been delivered from the rear.

Post-Mortem Trauma

Damage by animals presents a very different pattern and type of damage than does intentional dismemberment. Areas of destruction usually have more ragged edges. The actual impressions of teeth often can be seen. Different types of animals attack the body in different ways, therefore producing their own patterns of destruction. Small animals and birds may attack the corpse soon after death and begin with the most accessible of the soft tissue areas such as the eyes, lips, or ears. While much soft tissue may be lost, rarely are these kinds of carnivores able to do severe damage to the bones. However,

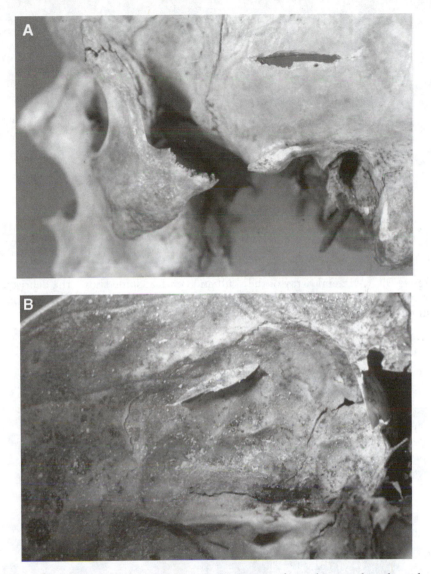

Figure 58   The exterior (A) and interior (B) view of a stab wound to the side of the skull. Note on the interior that the bone is bent as well as cut. (Photo courtesy of R.B. Pickering.)

even small animals may create small grooves or scratches on bone that might be confused with cut marks. Larger animals such as coyotes, dogs, and wolves, not to mention bears or mountain lions, are capable of consuming an entire body; however that does not mean that all bony evidence will be destroyed. Sometimes they will pierce, break, and gnaw bones. Small bones such as fingers or the thin bones on the shoulder blades may be very badly damaged and fragmented, and these small fragments are difficult to identify without

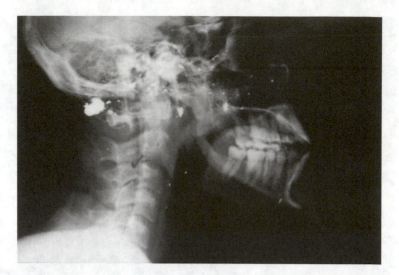

Figure 59 A lateral X-ray of the skull and cervical spine shows the debris path from a 9-mm bullet. (Photo courtesy of Triena Harper, Jefferson County Coroner's Office.)

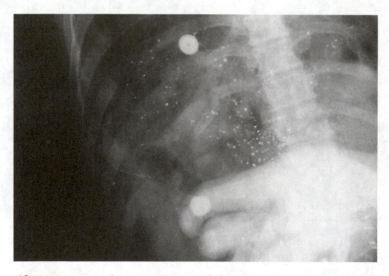

Figure 60 An anterior/posterior X-ray of the chest showing .30-06 bullet fragments that might be missed without a radiograph. (Photo courtesy of Triena Harper, Jefferson County Coroner's Office.)

proper training. Large bones may not be totally destroyed but often the ends of long bones, the portions that are helpful for identifying the specific bone, are chewed away. Unfortunately, these are the choicest areas from the carnivores' perspective because they hold rich marrow. The results are shaft fragments that may look similar between species (Figure 63). A large carnivore

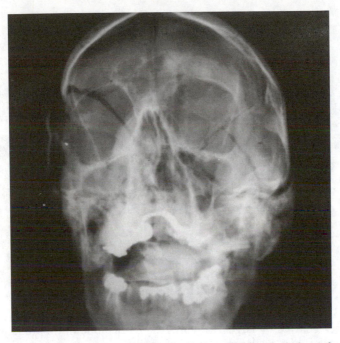

Figure 61 Multiple fractures to the skull show up as dark lines between the lighter colored bone. This particular injury resulted from massive blunt force. (Photo courtesy of Triena Harper, Jefferson County Coroner's Office.)

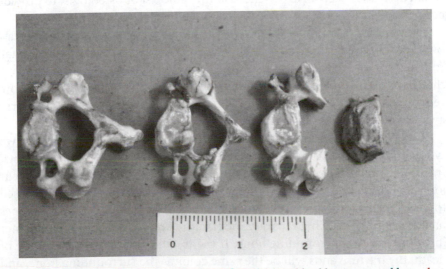

Figure 62 These neck vertebrae show that the head had been severed by a sharp instrument and also indicated the direction from which the blow came. (Photo courtesy of R.B. Pickering.)

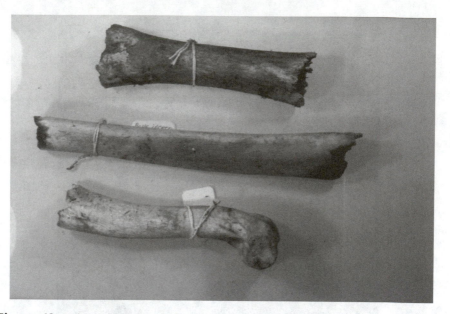

Figure 63 These bones were picked up by investigators at the recovery site. All had been gnawed by large carnivores. Only the bone in the middle is human. (Photo courtesy of R.B. Pickering.)

that scavenges a human carcass also hunts wild prey. Therefore, commingling of human and non-human remains may complicate the identification process. These cases need an experienced anthropologist or osteologist to provide accurate identification.

Scavenging doesn't stop when the soft tissue is gone. Rodents may gnaw on bones (Figure 64) leaving characteristic parallel incisor marks. While small rodents do not carry away large bones, they may feed on bone fragments that have been carried away by other scavengers. Birds scavenge hair from remains and may even carry away bones. Birds and packrats commonly carry away evidentiary materials such as keys, jewelry, or other shiny objects.

Besides animal scavenging, post-mortem trauma will generally be of two types: fractures that occur during recovery of the skeleton and incidental fractures unrelated to the case. Old bones are brittle and fractures that occur long after death may cause the bones to shatter. Bones that have been exposed to the elements for many weeks are usually stained a light brown. If the bones have been broken during recovery the fracture ends will be clean and lighter in color than the surrounding bone. If the fractures occurred at the time of death, the fracture ends will be the same color as the surrounding bone, and there is likely to be soil contamination in the fracture ends. In both instances the edges of the breaks will be sharp and irregular (Figure 65). Fractures that occurred during life and had some time to begin the healing process will be

Figure 64   Pairs of small parallel cuts result from rodent gnawing on this bone. The lighter color compared to the darker color of the adjacent bone means that the gnawing was recent. (Photo courtesy of R.B. Pickering.)

Figure 65   Bone fragments from the same skull may show different colors depending on preservation conditions. (Photo courtesy of R.B. Pickering.)

Figure 66   The fracture pattern on this skull indicates slow but heavy pressure. It is post-mortem trauma rather than peri-mortem. This skull was recovered from a grave in an old cemetery. (Photo courtesy of R.B. Pickering.)

rounded, showing evidence of healing. You'll need an expert, either a forensic pathologist or anthropologist, to make the determination of when the fracture occurred.

Post-mortem fractures can also occur in buried skeletons and have a characteristic appearance. A common example is remains from old wooden coffins that by accident or design become exposed. As the coffin disintegrates, heavy earth pressure is exerted on the skeleton, particularly the hollow skull. The result may be a deformed skull or one that has fracture lines along the sides of the cranial vault (Figure 66). When this occurs it looks as if part of the skull has been caved into the cranial cavity and the cavity is at least partially filled with dirt.

Pseudo-Trauma

Not all trauma is real. During the inventory of skeletal remains at the Denver Museum of Natural History that was made in compliance with NAGPRA, a skull with a puncture wound and an associated projectile point was examined (Figure 67). On initial inspection, it appeared that this man had been killed by a head wound when shot with an arrow. Closer examination, however, revealed that this was pseudo-trauma — someone had drilled this puncture wound in the skull to fit the projectile point making it appear to be a real

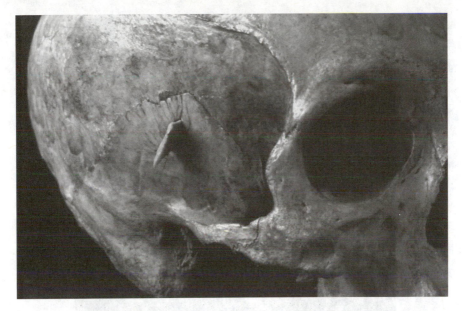

Figure 67   A case of pseudo-trauma in which a chert projectile point was inserted into the skull after death. (Photo courtesy of Rick Wicker/DMNH.)

wound. Again, it may take an expert to make the determination between real and pseudo-trauma.

Pathologic Changes in Bone

Trauma is not the only thing that leaves X-ray evidence of bony change that can lead to a positive identification. Everyone knows of the importance of dental X-rays in forensic cases. Skull films also have been used to make identifications. Frontal sinuses that are present in everyone's skull are diagnostic (Figure 68). The problem is that only a small minority of the population has had skull films taken during life that can be used for comparison.

Many diseases suffered during life leave telltale changes, many of them distinctive, on the skeleton. Pathology changes the normal to the abnormal and idiosyncratic. Identifying the abnormal helps separate the John Doe skeleton from all others. Congenital skeletal and developmental anomalies also may be useful. An archaeological case provides an excellent example. Careful examination of three different skeletons led to an almost certain conclusion that the three were genetically related. How could the anthropologist be so confident in his finding? Each of the three shared a common developmental anomaly — they all had two neck vertebrae that were fused together (Figure 69). A forensic anthropologist who examines skeletal

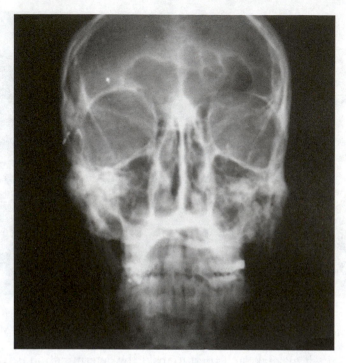

Figure 68   Anterior X-rays of the skull show the frontal sinus pattern which may be useful in comparing ante- and post-mortem radiographs. (Photo courtesy of Triena Harper, Jefferson County Coroner's Office.)

remains will be familiar with the conditions that leave such skeletal evidence. If a particular disease is suspected, the anthropologist may have to recruit another member for your investigative team — a physician who treats this disease in living people. Together these experts will be able tell you how a particular disease affected a person's life and how the affected person would look while alive. If you know that you are looking for a person with a particular appearance your investigation is narrowed. If you also know that a disease process significantly affected a person's behavior or physical life, you can assume that they have had significant medical care and that X-rays are probably available for comparison.

There is a long list of conditions that affect the skeleton, but some of the common ones and their distinguishing features are included here to stimulate your thinking about conditions that might help lead you to a positive identification.

One of these is arthritis, which alters the appearance of joints. Changes in extremity joints are much less distinctive than the changes that occur in the spine and, therefore, are too similar in appearance to make identification possible. Comparison of pre- and post-mortem X-rays of the spine, however, can make definitive identification. Virtually everyone over the age of 50 has

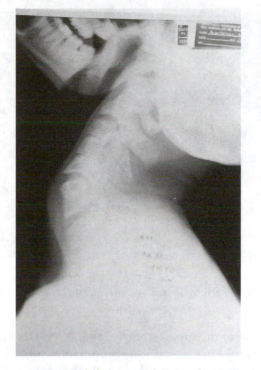

Figure 69 This lateral X-ray of the cervical spine shows congenitally fused 6th and 7th vertebrae. This kind of rare condition can help in determining identity. (Photo courtesy of James Quale, M.D., Swedish Medical Center.)

some degenerative disease in the spine and 80% of the population will have back pain sometime in their life. Many will have had back X-rays.

While it is true that the presence or absence of arthritic change can be a valuable trait for comparison with ante-mortem X-rays, that pattern of the arthritic change of the skeleton also can be useful when trying to determine the identity of the deceased. Arthritis tends to affect those joints that are used and abused the most. Therefore, the pattern of arthritis is an indicator of the type of activity of the person during life. Whether football player or ballerina, computer operator or jogger, the evidence of habitual activity or long term strenuous habits will be evidenced by some degenerative changes in the joints. Schmorl's nodules also are related to intense physical activity. They are protrusions of intervertebral disk material into the bones of adjacent vertebra. They are commonly found when examining skeletal remains and are seen on X-ray but are not distinctive enough to be useful in identification. An anthropologist knows how to identify each of these kinds of bony changes and to discern any pattern that might be there.

Many congenital anomalies (Figure 70) such as fused vertebra or hemivertebra will cause alterations in a person's appearance such as a short neck

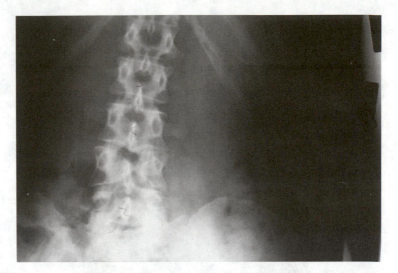

Figure 70   An anterior-posterior X-ray of the lumbar spine shows an unusual condition, "butterfly vertebra," of L-4. This anomaly is congenital. (Photo courtesy of James Quale, M.D., Swedish Medical Center.)

or lateral curvature of the spine (scoliosis) that is apparent in infancy or early childhood. Idiopathic scoliosis is a developmental problem that appears at about puberty (Figure 71). These abnormal curvatures will have been easily seen during life and these people will likely have had many X-rays.

Cervical ribs (extra ribs arising from cervical vertebra) (Figure 72) and bifurcated ribs (Figure 73) are distinctive, but seldom cause symptoms. Cervical ribs are always seen on chest X-rays, so if you can find a chest X-ray of a suspected victim you can make an identification.

Kyphosis or humpback can be caused by many things but is most common in older women who are osteoporotic and have had vertebral compression fractures. Most people with significant deformity will have had multiple episodes of medical care and distinctive X-rays.

Ankylosing spondylitis starts with low back pain, typically in young males. As it progresses, ligaments in the spine become ossified and a poker spine is the result. In a few cases the spine is erect, but in most cases the spine has a severe flexion deformity. The deformity, as well as X-rays of the spine, are unique in each person.

Infections of the spine, bacterial or tubercular, destroy disk spaces and the vertebral bodies. Each infection is unique and leaves distinctive X-ray changes (Figure 74). People who have had spinal infections will have been hospitalized for extended periods of time during their treatment and have many X-rays on file.

Osteomyelitis (bacterial infections) of bones of the extremities also leave distinctive marks (Figure 75). During active phases of the infections draining

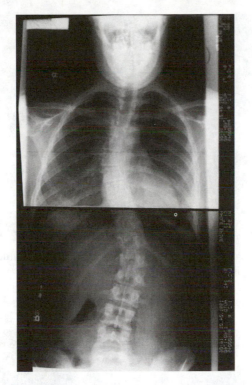

Figure 71   Idiopathic scoliosis of the spine presents an exaggerated curve from side to side. In its severe form, this condition can be seen easily in life. (Photo courtesy of James Quale, M.D., Swedish Medical Center.)

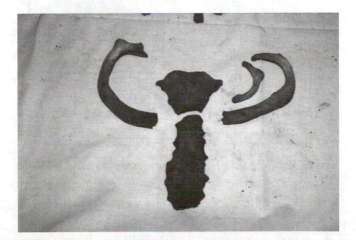

Figure 72   A cervical rib is an anomaly that should be visible on chest X-rays. The forensic anthropologist needs to determine if an extra rib found with a skeleton is a cervical rib or whether it represents a second individual. (Photo courtesy of R.B. Pickering.)

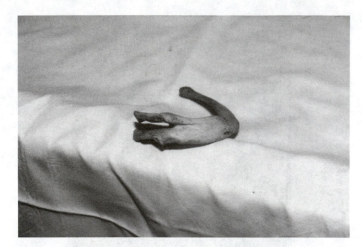

Figure 73 Bifurcated ribs also should be easily identifiable on chest X-rays. (Photo courtesy of R.B. Pickering.)

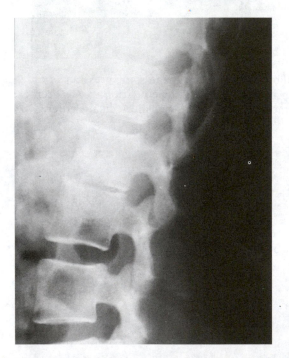

Figure 74 A lateral X-ray of the spine shows a disk space infection and osteomyelitis of the inferior portion of L-2 vertebral body. (Photo courtesy of James Quale, M.D., Swedish Medical Center.)

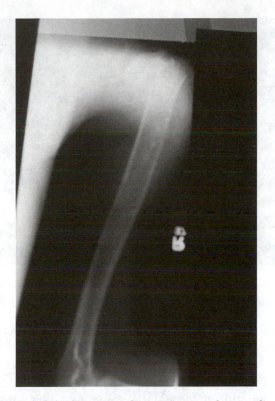

Figure 75   An X-ray of the humerus shows osteomyelitis with a fractured head. (Photo courtesy of James Quale, M.D., Swedish Medical Center.)

wounds will be present and, even if healing is attained, permanent bony deformity with permanent X-ray changes will persist.

Bone spurs usually occur near epiphyses of long bones. These bony prominences can be felt near the joints and are evident on X-rays. Bone cysts look distinctive on X-rays but may not cause any symptoms unless the bone fractures, a common occurrence because the cyst weakens the bone (Figure 76). The appearance of both spurs and cysts in bones may be unique enough to aid in identification.

Primary malignant tumors in bones are almost universally fatal. Treatment of these tumors is usually by amputation. Each amputation is unique. Metastatic cancer to bone leaves holes in the bones, visible on X-ray, that differ for each person.

Metabolic diseases such as gout or rickets produce bone changes that may not show X-ray changes different enough to aid in identification. Many other disease processes will leave their mark on the skeleton but are rare and often not helpful.

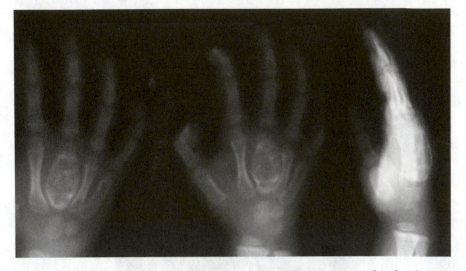

Figure 76 This dramatic set of X-rays presents a bone cyst on the third metacarpal of the hand. (Photo courtesy of James Quale, M.D., Swedish Medical Center.)

In summary, congenital abnormalities and disease processes that affect bones during life can leave permanent changes on the skeleton that can aid in narrowing an investigation for the possible identity of victims. If you find significant deformities on skeletal remains, it is probable that this person had significant problems during life and that someone, either family or a medical specialist, is going to know about those problems. If you are lucky, someone will have recorded these problems on medical records and with X-rays.

If the skeletal remains you are investigating has significant bony abnormalities, you have made a positive first step in identifying your subject. Get your forensic anthropologist and physician together to tell you how these bony changes would have affected your subject during life. You want to know how this person looked during life and what any acquaintances would have seen. If they tell you that your subject had a severely deformed spine you have specific questions to ask during your investigation.

Follow-Up Steps for Skeletal Abnormalities

1. Document all evidence of skeletal abnormalities with good photographs.
2. X-ray all skeletal remains to look for evidence of trauma or disease.
3. Separate ante-, peri-, and post-mortem trauma.
4. Use your outside experts to tell you what effect skeletal changes would have on a person during life.
5. Use this information to narrow your field of investigation.

Putting Your
Case Together

9

Let's go back to our original case, John Brown's body. You've gathered all of the information, now what are you going to do with it? The district attorney as well as the press are anxious to have some answers. Who was this person? When did death occur? Was it homicide? What's your evidence and can it stand up in court? Should the DA be considering charges against somebody?

You have found some answers. This is a case of complete skeletal remains found in the woods. You know these are not ancient remains because your subject was wearing jeans and 1984 coins were found with the body. Your subject must have died during or after 1984.

The consulting forensic anthropologist made a complete inventory of the remains at the scene before the skeleton was removed and found that all the bones were present. After thorough evaluation in the lab, your anthropologist told you that the subject was an adult Caucasian male, aged 20–30, and 5-ft-8-in. to 5-ft-10-in. tall. X-rays of your subject's right ankle showed that he fractured this ankle sometime as an adult. There is a screw in the medial malleolus. The X-ray of this ankle could lead to a probable identification if ante-mortem X-rays can be found for comparison. Rodents have done minimal damage to the bones, but there is evidence of gnawing. There is no carnivore damage.

The consulting forensic odontologist told you that your subject has had all four third molars pulled and has fillings in the upper right first molar and the lower left second molar. He X-rayed the teeth and will be able to make a positive identification if X-rays are located for comparison. Completed root formation of the teeth indicates that this subject was more than 25 years old.

The forensic anthropologist found more than just the coins and jeans material during the scene investigation. Two bullets, which your ballistic expert identified as 30-30 caliber, were discovered under the skeletal remains when the ground was screened. There was a comminuted fracture of the left fifth rib posteriorly with some bullet fragments that can be seen on X-rays of the subject. Close evaluation of this fracture in the rib indicates that this was caused by a bullet entering posteriorly. Exit of the bullet must have been anteriorly through the costal cartilage which is no longer present. This discovery of bullets with fragments in the rib raises the suspicion that your subject died from gunshot wounds.

Because these remains were completely skeletonized with no flesh adhering to the bones, no entomologist was called. If soft tissue had been found on the skeleton an entomologist could have provided additional information about time of death.

A botanist from the local university examined the remains before removal and told you that death had to have occurred more than two years previously, based on plant growth in and around the skeleton.

At this point you know that a 5-ft-8 in. to 5-ft-10-in. adult Caucasian male aged 25–30 died more than 2 and less than 13 years ago. Other information you learned from your investigation opens some avenues for speculation. The scene where your subject was found is important. The scene is in a forested area at an elevation of 2200 feet, 10 miles southwest of the nearest town. An old farm road runs through the area and the body was found 50 yards from this road. Several farms surround this forested area and the nearest buildings are one quarter mile northwest of the site where the subject was discovered.

The local wildlife officer told you that bird hunting is common in the area. Bird hunting is almost universally done with shotguns, not rifles. Deer are rarely found in this area so large caliber rifle hunting would be unlikely. With homes near the area, target shooting with large caliber rifles would be unwelcome and would draw attention. Officers from your department have interviewed nearby residents who have no recollection of frequent gunfire in the area.

Your forensic anthropologist has given you one additional piece of information. When discovered, your subject was lying face down with his legs extended and his arms straight at his side. If your subject was killed by gunshot wounds it was probably intentional, not accidental. Your subject must have been shot at the scene while lying prone. It is probable that 30-30 bullets would have passed through his body. If he was standing or was shot elsewhere these bullets would not have been found directly under the skeletal remains. This evidence points to homicide.

With this information in hand your search of missing persons records on the NCIC computer turns up 50 undiscovered Caucasian male subjects, age 25–30, who disappeared in this country over the past 13 years. Since five of them disappeared in your state you requested their records as the first step. Review of the dental records by the odontologist and X-rays by the forensic anthropologist and a radiologist produce a match with a 27-year-old male who was reported missing 6 years ago in a city 20 miles away.

Your final report to the district attorney identifies your subject as Eustace Hinklemuff whose last known address was 1234 Main Street, Gotham Center. His long criminal record identifies him as a drug dealer with multiple arrests. It is your opinion that his death was due to homicide by an unknown assailant or assailants at the location where his remains were discovered.

Further investigation of the missing person case and narcotic division records in the Gotham Center Police Department produces information that your victim had been involved in a dispute with two known drug dealers who were attempting to take over the territory controlled by your victim. These two people were arrested.

Since your investigation was thoroughly documented, your evidence and identification confirmed by your expert's testimony was completely accepted at the trial. After additional testimony by associates of the victim and the accused, the jury began deliberation.

This scenario illustrates the way in which a forensic anthropologist can help you in solving a complex case that involves skeletal remains. In this case, the consulting forensic anthropologist provided essential information that led to the solution of a homicide.

Closing the Case, Closing the Book

Every death investigation raises three questions: Who is this person? When did this person die? What caused this person's death? Most of the time these answers are clear and straightforward. But even in apparently obvious situations the investigation can rarely be completed by a single person; additional experts are usually needed to give final answers to these three questions.

In a witnessed death at least some of the questions have readily apparent answers. Because the death is observed the time can be documented and most of the time, identification can be made by the witnesses. In cases where the person is unknown to the witnesses, identification usually can be made from personal effects such as driver's license or similar forms.

The cause in sudden, unexpected deaths requires investigation by a pathologist. A forensic pathologist, trained to identify causes of death due to violence, will be best able to give answers in situations where criminal activity is suspected. Even in deaths due to motor vehicle accidents, an autopsy is indicated. Was the accident caused by a heart attack or stroke? Was the accident due to drug or alcohol intoxication?

In unwitnessed deaths the problem becomes more complicated. Identification usually can still be made from personal effects such as I.D. cards with photos. When no personal effects are found, fingerprinting of the deceased often can lead to identification. Visual identification by associates of the deceased is possible as long as the death is recent and decomposition has not advanced.

Time of death is more uncertain. The only thing known with certainty is that death occurred between the time the person was last seen alive and the time the body was discovered. The condition of the body may help the coroner or medical examiner narrow the time further.

Cause of death determination absolutely depends on a forensic autopsy. These deaths are homicides until proven otherwise. Even apparent motor vehicle accidents can mask homicides or suicides.

In deaths involving a badly decomposed body or skeletal remains the degree of difficulty increases geometrically. With loss of facial features and finger skin for fingerprints, identification will only be possible with skilled technical assistance. Even if I.D. cards are present with the body, corroboration that this material belongs to the deceased is necessary.

A forensic odontologist can furnish that positive corroboration if antemortem dental X-rays are available for comparison with the X-rays made at autopsy. If no films for comparison are available, then other expertise will be required, but chances of absolute identification diminish.

A forensic pathologist's examination of a decomposed body may yield little information if the internal organs are gone. In most cases the pathologist will ask a forensic anthropologist to perform an additional examination.

If the only thing remaining of the body is the skeleton, then examination by a forensic anthropologist is your only chance of finding answers to the three questions listed above. There are two ways to seek answers from a forensic anthropologist. One way is by recruiting a bunch of people to go out to the scene and gather up all the bones you can find. You may end up with the jawbone of an ass and a rabbit's femur that someone thought was a metatarsal or you may miss some of the essential bones from your skeleton. Once this is done, you can box up everything you find and send it to an expert somewhere. This expert will be able to reconstruct the skeleton, and if enough bones are present he should be able to give you an indication of the race, sex, age, and stature of the deceased.

That's often the way it had to be done in the past. Now there's a second and better way. Instead of picking up the remains yourself, you can get a forensic anthropologist to accompany you to the scene to recover the skeletal remains. There are enough qualified forensic anthropologists across the country that you should be able to locate one in your region. That, of course, requires some planning. You need to identify and establish a relationship with a qualified forensic anthropologist before the need for one arises. All Members or Fellows of the American Academy of Forensic Sciences are listed in the AAFS Directory.

What can you expect from a forensic anthropologist at the scene? You can expect two things: one, finding all the bones from the skeletal remains and two, reconstructing the context at the site. This is particularly important if the remains are scattered or burned. Your forensic anthropologist also will be able to tell whether more than one body is present. That information would be nice to know before you ship the bones off because it will change your investigation. More than that, the positioning of the remains may yield valuable clues to the circumstances of death.

Let's go back to our scenario of John Brown's body. An expert to whom you sent a box of bones would not immediately know that the remains were lying face down when found. If you sent adequate photos of the scene along with the bones the expert could figure that out, but that important clue would be immediately known by your forensic anthropologist at the scene. The finding of posterior rib fractures on the remains caused by gunshot injuries would lead the forensic anthropologist at the scene to search for bullets, which were ultimately found under the remains indicating that death occurred at that site. The expert looking at your box of bones would know that there was a gunshot injury, but the chance of finding the bullets under the remains would have been lost.

A laboratory examination by a forensic anthropologist will be directed toward identifying the race, sex, age, and stature of the deceased person. The ability to make these determinations depends on the completeness of the remains; the more complete the remains the more certain the determination. By working at the scene, a forensic anthropologist can tell you immediately if the remains are complete and can help you find scattered remains if they are not. A local wildlife officer can be an additional resource in finding scattered remains. This person should be asked to come to the scene before the bones are picked up because the pattern of scatter may point to a predator that carried the missing bones. The wildlife officer will be of help in this instance as he will usually understand the habits of each predator in the area.

Knowing the race, sex, age, and stature of the deceased person does not mean that you have identified that person. If the forensic anthropologist finds individual skeletal anomalies or pathology, they can help make the identification if ante-mortem medical records can be matched with the post-mortem findings.

Time of death in decomposed and fully skeletonized remains is often impossible to determine. A forensic anthropologist can help determine a range of time by finding artifacts that give information about when the deceased was still alive. Additional experts such as an entomologist and botanist also can provide a range of time that the remains were present at the site by studying the insect infestation and plant growth around the remains. If you can identify the skeletal remains you can narrow the range for time of death to the period between the time the person was last seen alive and the time when the remains was discovered.

The cause of death in decomposing and skeletonized remains is usually difficult to determine. If you are lucky and enough soft tissue is present on decomposing skeletal remains, a forensic pathologist may discover the cause. In fully skeletonized remains a forensic anthropologist may find subtle changes on the bones that identify the kind of trauma that caused the death. A forensic toxicologist may discover poisons or drugs that produced death. In many cases the cause will never be discovered.

There are some important steps you can take to facilitate your investigation of decomposing and skeletonized remains. The following are major points of emphasis made in this book.

1. Investigation of semi-skeletal or skeletal remains requires a team approach. You cannot do the investigation by yourself.
2. Make certain that you do a complete investigation.
3. Don't move the body before your investigation is complete.
4. A qualified forensic anthropologist is your best resource for identifying skeletal remains.
5. Bring whatever expertise you need to the scene.
6. Identify the experts you may need for a skeletal recovery as part of your preplanning.
7. Establish ground rules with your experts on how they will help you before the investigation begins.
8. Plan in advance for what basic equipment will be needed.
9. Photograph and videotape every phase of the investigation.
10. Keep meticulous records. Your testimony in court will only be as good as your records. Memory is fallible.

Bibliography

Goldstein, J. L. and Brown, M. S., *Harrison's Principles of Internal Medicine*, 12th Edition, McGraw Hill, New York, NY, 1991, p. 22.

Orthopaedic Knowledge Update-I, American Academy of Orthopaedic Surgeons, Chicago, IL, 1984.

Bass, W. M. Time interval since death, in *Human Identification*, Rathbun, T. A. and Buikstra, J. E. (Eds.), Charles C Thomas, Springfield, IL, 1984, pp. 136-142.

Brady, W. J. *Outline of Death Investigation*, Oregon State Medical Examiners Office, 1982, p. 41.

Catts, E.P. and Haskell, N. H. *Entomology and Death: A Procedural Guide*, Joyce's Print Shop, Inc., Clemson, SC, 1990, chapter 8.

Dwight, T. *The Identification of Human Skeleton. A Medicolegal Study* (prize essay, Massachusetts Medical Society) Boston, MA 1878.

Farley, M. A. and Harrington, J. J. (Eds.) *Forensic DNA Technology*, Lewis Publishers, Chelsea, MI, 1991, chapter 3.

Iscan, M. Y. and Kennedy, K. A. R. *Reconstruction of Life from the Skeleton*, Alan R. Liss, New York, NY, 1989, pp. 238, 253.

Kerley, E. Recent developments in forensic anthropology, in *Yearbook of Physical Anthropology*, American Association of Physical Anthropologists, Volume 21, 1978, pp. 160-173.

Klonaris, N. S. and Furue, T., 1980 Photographic Superimposition in Dental Identification. Is a Picture Worth a Thousand Words? *Journal of Forensic Sciences*, 25(4), 1980, pp. 859-865.

Krogman, W. M. A Guide to the Identification of Human Skeletal Material, in *FBI Law Enforcement Bulletin*, 8(8): 3-31, 1939.

Krogman, W. M. *The Human Skeleton in Forensic Medicine*, Charles C Thomas, Springfield, IL, 1962.

Krogman, W. M. *The Human Skeleton in Forensic Medicine*, second edition, Charles C Thomas, Springfield, IL, 1973, pp. 129, 155, 190.

Leske, G. S., Repa, L. W. and Leske, M. C., Dental public health in *Public Health and Preventive Medicine*, 11th edition, Last, J.M. (Ed.), Appleton-Century-Crofts, New York, NY, 1980, p. 1460.

Joe Levisky, M.D. Personal Communication, 1995.

Maples, W. R. and Browning, M. *Dead Men Do Tell Tales*, Doubleday, New York, NY, 1994, pp. 233-236.

Maxcy-Rosenau, X. X. Dental public health, in *Public Health and Preventive Medicine*, 11th Edition, Last, J. M. (Ed.), Appleton-Century-Crofts, New York, NY, 1980, chapter 43.

McKern, T. W. and Stewart, T. D. *Skeletal Age Changes in Young American Males*, Environmental Protection Research Division (Quartermaster Research And Development Center, U.S. Army, Natick, MA, Technical Report EP-45 1957.

Pickering, R. B. and Frohman E. M., *Determining the ABO Blood Group of Hair and Fingernail Specimens through the Absorption-Elution Technique*. Paper presented at the annual meeting of the American Academy of Forensic Sciences. 1977.

Rethers, H. F. *History of the American Graves Registration Service, Q. M. C. in Europe*, Volume I, Office of the Quartermaster General, n.d.

Snow, D. G. Forensic anthropology, in *Anthropology Beyond the University*, A. Redfield, (Ed.), Southern Anthropological Society Proceedings, No. 7, 4-17, n.d.

Steele, D. G. Estimation of stature from fragments of long limb bones, in *Personal Identification in Mass Disasters*, T. D. Stewart (Ed.), National Museum of Natural History, Washington, D.C., 1970, pp. 85-97.

Stewart, T. D. *Essentials of Forensic Anthropology*, Charles C Thomas Press, Springfield, IL, 1979.

Thomson, H. *Murder at Harvard*, Houghton-Mifflin Company, Boston, MA 1971.

Wuehrmann, A. H. and Manson-Hing, L. R. *Dental Radiology*, second edition, C. V. Mosby, St. Louis, MO, 1969, p. 258.

Glossary

While not all of these words may appear in this book, they may appear in medical reports that you receive. Having these definitions will help you understand these reports.

Acetabulum   Pelvic socket for the head of the femur (hip socket).

Acromion   Part of the scapular bone that forms the point of the shoulder.

Adipocere   Brown, wax-like substance composed of fatty acids and calcium soaps produced by the terminal decomposition of a body.

Anomaly   Deviation from normal; something contrary to the general rule or to what is expected.

Ante-mortem   Before death.

Anterior   Before or in front of.

Anthropology   The study of humans and their cultures.

Apophysis   A projection from bone without an independent center of ossification.

Archaeology   Study of extinct human civilizations.

Arthritis   Inflammation of a joint, usually accompanied by pain, swelling, and changes in structure.

Artifact   Anything artificially produced; a simple man-made object.

Astragalus   Old term for talus; ball of ankle joint.

Biological   Pertaining to the science of life and living things.

Biological degradation   Breakdown of organic materials into simple chemicals by biochemical processes.

Calcaneus (os calcis)   Heel bone.

Calvarium   Dome-like superior portion of the cranium.

Carpus (carpal bones)   The eight bones of the wrist joint.

Caudal   Toward the tail, in a posterior direction.

Cervical   In the region of the neck.

Clavicle   Collar bone.

Coccyx   Tail bone.

Comminuted   Broken in more than two pieces.

Condyle   A rounded protuberance at the end of a bone forming a portion of the joint.

Congenital   Present at birth.

Coracoid process   Process on upper anterior surface of scapula.

Coronal plane   Plane dividing the body into front and back portions.

Corpus   Principal part of any organ; any mass or body.

Costal   Pertaining to a rib.

Cranium   That portion of the skull that encloses the brain.

Crest   A ridge or elongated prominence on a bone.

Cuboid   One of the tarsal bones.

Degenerative   Deterioration of an organ or structure such as a joint.

Dentition   The type, number, and arrangement of teeth in the dental arch.

Diaphysis   The shaft or middle part of a long cylindrical bone.

Digit   A finger or toe.

Distal   Farthest from the center, a medial line, or the trunk, anatomically — of the end of any structure.

DNA   Deoxyribonucleic acid; chemical basis of heredity, the carrier of genetic information.

Ectocranial   Outside of the cranium.

Entomology   The study of insects.

Epiphysis   The center of bone growth at the end of long bones, separated from the rest of the bone in early life by cartilage.

Ethmoid bone   Bone that forms the roof of the nasal fossa and part of the floor of the anterior fossa of the skull.

External   On the outside of the body.

Femur   Thigh bone.

Fibula   The smaller of the two lower leg bones.

Fontanel   The soft spot lying between the cranial bones of a fetus.

Foramen   A hole in a bone for the passage of vessels or nerves.

Forensic   Pertaining to the law, legal.

Fossa   A furrow or shallow depression.

Fracture   A broken or cracked bone.

Frontal   Anterior.

Frontal bone   Forehead bone.

Genu   Pertaining to the knee.

Head   Proximal end of any bone; the skull.

Hematoma   A mass of blood (usually clotted) in an organ, tissue, or space.

Hemivertebra   Congenital absence of half a vertebra.

Humerus   Upper arm bone.

Hyoid bone   Horseshoe-shaped bone lying at the base of the tongue consisting of a left wing, body, and right wing.

Idiopathic   Condition without recognizable cause.

Ilium   One of the three bones that make up the innominate bone; the superior and widest part.

Inferior   Beneath, lower, below.

Innominate bone   One of the three fused bones, the ilium, ischium, and pubis, that make up part of the pelvis.

Internal   Within the body.

Intervertebral disk   Broad or flattened disk of fibrocartilage between the bodies of the vertebrae.

Intracranial   Inside the cranium.

Ischium   Lower portion of the innominate bone.

Kyphosis   Exaggeration of the normal posterior curve of the spine; hunchback.

Lip   A lip-like structure forming the border of an opening or groove.

Lumbar   The lower back between the thorax and pelvis.

Mandible   Lower jaw.

Manubrium   Upper portion of the sternum or breast bone.

Mastoid   Prominent process of the temporal bone located just behind the ear.

Maxilla   Upper jaw bone.

Medial   Toward the middle.

Medicolegal   Related to medical jurisprudence or forensic medicine.

Metacarpals   Bones of the hand.

Metaphysis   Portion of bone between the diaphysis and epiphysis.

Metatarsal   Bones of the forefoot.

Metastatic   Secondary growth of a malignancy in a new location.

Morphology   Science of structure and form without regard to function.

Nasal   Pertaining to the nose.

Navicular   Bone in the wrist and mid-foot.

Obturator foramen   Opening on each side of the front of the pelvis.

Occipital bone   Bone in the back part of the skull.

Occiput   The back part of the skull.

Odontologist   A dentist or dental surgeon.

Olecranon   Point of the elbow; proximal end of the ulna.

Orbit   The bony cavity that contains and protects the eyeball.

Ossification   Formation of bone.

Osteology   The science of structure and function of bone.

Osteomyelitis   Infection in bone.

Palate   The roof of the mouth including both the bony hard palate and the soft palate.

Parietal bone   One of the two bones that together form the roof and sides of the skull.

Pathology   Study of the nature and cause of disease.

Pelvic inlet   Upper pelvic entrance.

Pelvis   The bony structure formed by the innominate bones, sacrum, and coccyx.

Peri-mortem   At or around the time of death.

Periosteum   The fibrous sleeve that surrounds bone.

Phalanges   Bones of a finger or toe.

Posterior   Toward the rear.

Post-mortem   After death.

Process   A projection or outgrowth of bone.

Prosthesis   Replacement of a missing part by an artificial substitute.

Proximal   Nearest the point of attachment, center of the body, or point of reference.

Pseudo   Prefix meaning false.

Pubis   Anterior part of the innominate bone.

Radius   The outer and shorter forearm bone.

Sacrum   The triangular bone at the base of the spine normally made up of five fused vertebra.

Sacroiliac joint   The joint between the innominate bone and the sacrum.

Sagittal plane   Anterior-posterior plane that divides the body into right and left halves.

Scapula   Shoulder blade.

Sciatic notch   Posterior indentation of innominate bone that separates the ilium and ischium.

Scoliosis   Lateral curvature of the spine.

Sinus   A cavity within a bone.

Skull   The bony framework of the head, composed of 8 cranial bones, 14 facial bones, and the teeth.

Spine   A sharp process of bone; the spinal column consists of 33 vertebrae: 7 cervical, 12 thoracic, 5 lumbar, 5 sacral, and 4 coccygeal.

Sternum   The breast bone.

Superficial   Confined to the surface.

Superior   Situated above something else; higher than.

Supraorbital   Above the orbit.

Talus   The ankle bone articulating with the tibia, fibula, calcaneus, and navicular.

Tarsal bones   The seven bones which make up the mid- and hind-foot.

Temporal bone   A bone on both sides of the skull.

Thorax   The rib cage and chest cavity.

Tibia   The shin bone.

Trochanter   Either of two bony processes below the neck of the femur.

Tubercle   A small rounded elevation on a bone.

Tuberosity   An elevated round process on a bone.

Ulna   The inner, longer forearm bone.

Ventral   Pertaining to the anterior or front portion of the body.

Vertebra   Any one of the 33 bony segments of the spinal column.

Vertex   The top of the head.

Xiphoid process   The lowest portion of the sternum.

Zygomatic bone   Cheekbone, the bone on either side of the face below the eye.

APPENDIX: Report Forms

- Humans Remains Investigation: Cover Sheet
- Humans Remains Investigation: Forensic Anthropology Summary
- Humans Remains Investigation: General Information
- Humans Remains Investigation: Contextual Description
- Humans Remains Investigation: Recovery Area
- Humans Remains Investigation: General Description of Remains
- Humans Remains Investigation: Inventory
- Humans Remains Investigation: Photo and Video Inventory

The following report forms are suggestions for your use.

Nothing in these forms is permanent; it is written on a computer therefore easily changeable. Use them in any way that is helpful to you. You may use them as presented or modify them in any way that suits your needs.

The important thing is to be prepared and have report forms ready to use the next time you must investigate a case of human remains. The principal reason to have prepared forms is to help you make certain that you have covered every facet of the case during your investigation. It is easy to forget things in the heat of the moment. If you have a form asking about each step in the case you are forced to answer that question and your investigation is more likely to be complete.

Standardized forms allow agencies to transfer information back and forth in a manner that minimizes the chances of misinterpretation. In addition, you will have recorded that information and it will be available for your review and testimony if the case goes to trial. The value of your testimony will be based solely on what you can document with your records.

Human Remains Investigation: Cover Sheet

This report provides a summary of your investigation. It identifies the case jurisdiction, the lead investigator, when and who reported the remains, where they were located, who worked on the case from other agencies, the identification of the remains, and their final disposition.

A key feature is the assigned case number. This should be assigned by the jurisdiction in which the case is located. It must be the same number for every report form and for every agency assisting in the investigation. If different agencies use different numbers the chances for confusion and loss of clues and data increase.

HUMAN REMAINS INVESTIGATION: COVER SHEET

JURISDICTION:
CASE NUMBER:
INVESTIGATOR IN CHARGE: PHONE:
DATE OF INITIAL REPORT:
REPORTING PARTY:
LOCATION OF REMAINS:
AGENCIES INVOLVED/INVESTIGATOR/PHONE NUMBER
    Sheriff's office:
    Police department:
    District Attorney's office:
    State agency:
    Federal agency:
    Other:
CONSULTANTS/PHONE NUMBER
    Forensic anthropologist:
    Forensic pathologist:
    Forensic odontologist:
    Entomologist:
    Botanist:
    Other:
IDENTIFICATION OF REMAINS
    Subject:
    By: Date:
    Method:
FINAL DISPOSITION:

Human Remains Investigation: Forensic Anthropology Summary

This is the summary that you want your forensic anthropology consultant to provide. This report identifies specific physical information about your subject and allows you to compare it to information about a suspected victim.

Using our example of John Brown's body, you can compare what the anthropologist tells you about the remains with the information you have about a missing subject. This information should assist you in making a positive identification of the remains.

SUBJECT INFORMATION	SUSPECTED VICTIM
SUBJECT NUMBER: 1	SUBJECT NUMBER: 1
CULTURAL AFFILIATION: Caucasian	CULTURAL AFFILIATION: Caucasian
SEX: Male	SEX: Male
AGE: 25–30	AGE: 27
STATURE: 5'8"–5'10"	STATURE: 5'8"
INDIVIDUAL CHARACTERISTICS: all third molars absent; right upper first molar filling; left lower third molar filling; old right ankle fracture; with malleolar screw	INDIVIDUAL CHARACTERISTICS: all third molars absent; right upper first molar filling; left lower third molar filling; old right ankle fracture; with malleolar screw

Human Remains Investigation: Forensic Anthropology Summary

JURISDICTION:

CASE NUMBER:

INVESTIGATOR IN CHARGE: PHONE:

FORENSIC ANTHROPOLOGIST:

REMAINS RECOVERY DATE:

REMAINS RECOVERY SITE:

SUBJECT INFORMATION   SUSPECTED VICTIM

   Subject number:

   Cultural affiliation: Cultural affiliation:

   Sex: Sex:

   Age: Age:

   Stature: Stature:

   Individual characteristics: Individual characteristics:

IDENTIFICATION:

   Subject Name:

   Date:

   By:

   Method:

Human Remains Investigation: General Information

This form inventories the personal effects and artifacts from the scene of the discovered remains and identifies the repository of the remains, personal effects, and artifacts. We have all had experience with relatives claiming that the victim's $10,000 diamond ring is missing. A record of the inventory of all personal effects found at the scene protects you from spurious claims. Specific identification of the repository of these effects is important when you are trying to locate them two years after the fact.

HUMAN REMAINS INVESTIGATION: GENERAL INFORMATION

JURISDICTION:

CASE NUMBER:

INVESTIGATOR IN CHARGE: PHONE:

THIS REPORT COMPLETED BY: DATE:

DATE REMAINS REPORTED:

DATE REMAINS RECOVERED:

IDENTIFICATION OF REMAINS IF KNOWN:

REPOSITORY OF REMAINS:

INVENTORY OF CLOTHING: BY:

REPOSITORY OF CLOTHING:

INVENTORY OF PERSONAL EFFECTS: BY:

REPOSITORY OF PERSONAL EFFECTS:

INVENTORY OF ADDITIONAL ARTIFACTS FROM SITE: BY:

REPOSITORY OF ARTIFACTS:

Human Remains Investigation: Contextual Description

This form identifies the site of and access to the discovered remains. The altitude, micro environment, and vegetation zone are important features that may assist in determining how long the remains have been at the site.

HUMAN REMAINS INVESTIGATION: CONTEXTUAL DESCRIPTION

JURISDICTION:
CASE NUMBER:
INVESTIGATOR IN CHARGE: PHONE:
SEARCH AREA:
   LOCATION OF REMAINS:

   ACCESS TO AREA:

   ALTITUDE:

MICROENVIRONMENT:

VEGETATION ZONE: (circle one)
   Forest   Swamp
   Grassland   City
   Cleared Land

NEARBY ARCHITECTURAL FEATURES:

ANIMAL ACTIVITY:

NOTES:

Human Remains Investigation: Recovery Area

This form records information about the specific recovery area and identifies consultants who may have taken samples from the site.

Evidence of post-mortem animal and human disturbance helps separate changes that occurred after deposition of the remains from things that happened at the time of death, which may help determine the cause and manner of death.

HUMAN REMAINS INVESTIGATION: RECOVERY AREA

JURISDICTION:

CASE NUMBER:

INVESTIGATOR IN CHARGE: PHONE:

DATE OF RECOVERY:

RECOVERY BY:

LOCATION OR RECOVERY AREA:

ALTITUDE:

MICRO ENVIRONMENT:

EXPOSURE TO SUNLIGHT:

TEMPERATURE RANGE FOR AREA:

GROUND COVER:

SURROUNDING VEGETATION:

SOIL SAMPLE:

   Taken by: Phone:

   Laboratory:

INSECT SAMPLES:

   Live   Dead

   Taken by: Phone:

   Laboratory:

EVIDENCE OF POST-MORTEM ANIMAL OR HUMAN DISTURBANCE:

EVIDENCE OF PERI-MORTEM HUMAN DISTURBANCE:

Human Remains Investigation: General Description of Remains

This report is important for two reasons. If completely filled out it makes certain that the remains and their disposition at the site are fully described. This record may be essential for your testimony in court later. Your forensic anthropologist should fill this out at the scene.

If for some reason you have failed to ask a forensic anthropologist to help you recover the remains and you suddenly appear with a bag of bones, this information will help the anthropologist who performs the laboratory investigation on those remains. You will have a second class investigation but it is better than you would get if you presented no information at all.

HUMAN REMAINS INVESTIGATION:
GENERAL DESCRIPTION OF REMAINS

JURISDICTION:

CASE NUMBER:

INVESTIGATOR IN CHARGE: PHONE:

DATE OF RECOVERY:

PROBABLE NUMBER OF REMAINS: (circle one)
  Single
  Multiple number
  Indeterminant commingled remains

MODE OF DISPOSITION OF REMAINS (circle one)
  On surface
  Exposed
  Covered with
  In vehicle   In building
  Buried (depth)
  Partially buried
  Was disposition: (circle one)
    Accidental   Intentional   Unknown
  Evidence of restraint:

INTEGRITY OF REMAINS: (circle one)
  Complete body   Partially skeletal   Skeletal
  Description:

COMPLETENESS OF REMAINS: (circle one)
  Complete and intact   Complete but disarticulated   Incomplete

HUMAN REMAINS INVESTIGATION:
GENERAL DESCRIPTION OF REMAINS

JURISDICTION:

CASE NUMBER:

DEGREE OF DECOMPOSITION: (circle one)

   No/minimal decomposition

   Bloating/discoloration

   Major soft tissue decomposition

   Remains mostly skeletonized

   Remains completely skeletonized

   Skeletal deterioration

EVIDENCE OF CREMATION: (circle one)

   LOCATION: *In situ*   Other location

   EVIDENCE: Burned soil or vegetation   Accelerant

   SAMPLES TAKEN:

     By: Phone:

     Laboratory:

BODY ORIENTATION (axis of body):

BODY POSITION (e.g., prone, supine, flexed on side — right/left)

LIMB ORIENTATION: STRAIGHT   DEGREE OF FLEXION

   Head

   Right arm

   Left arm

   Right leg

   Left leg

   Hand position: right

               left

NOTES:

Human Remains Investigation: Inventory

Everything should be inventoried: the remains, the clothing, the personal effects, and any other items found at the scene. The persons doing the inventory should identified. In most cases. It is wise to have two people doing the inventory, particularly if there are valuable items involved. Every inventoried item should be identified by number and recorded on separate sheets for remains, clothing, personal effects, and other items.

HUMAN REMAINS INVESTIGATION: INVENTORY

JURISDICTION:
CASE NUMBER:
BY: DATE:

LABEL EVERY ITEM WITH APPROPRIATE IDENTIFICATION TAGS
Number   Description

                                    Remains
                                    Clothing
                                    Personal effects
                                    Other items

Human Remains Investigation: Photo and Video Inventory

Photograph and videotape as much of your investigation as you can. Make sure that you make a record of everything that you do photograph. This can form a permanent record of your investigation that may be invaluable at a trial as it documents what you have done.

HUMAN REMAINS INVESTIGATION: PHOTO AND VIDEO INVENTORY

JURISDICTION:
CASE NUMBER:
INVESTIGATOR IN CHARGE: PHONE:
PHOTOGRAPHS

Number	Description	Date	Time	By

VIDEOS

Number	Description	Date	Time	By

Index

A

ABO blood typing, 115–116
Absorption-elution technique, 115–116
Academic qualifications, 26–27
Age determination, 86–91
    case report examples, 37, 40, 42
    by degenerative change, 90
    by dentition, 88
    by epiphyseal growth, 87
    for fractures, 128–129
    by osteon counting, 113–114
    by pubic symphysis, 89–90
    by skull, 88–89
Agreement, letters of, 32, 33
Algor mortis, 98
Altered remains, *see* Postmortem disturbance
Amateur recovery, 53–56, 142
American Academy of Forensic Sciences (AAFS),
    5, 25–26
American blacks, sexual dimorphism in, 83
American Revolution, 1
Amputation, 94–95, 137
Animals
    pets, 50–53
    scavenging behavior, 49–50, 55, 101, 123–128,
        140
Ankylosing spondylitis, 134
Antemortem trauma, 119–122, *see also*
        Postmortem disturbance
Anthropologist, *see also* Forensic anthropologist
    forensic defined, 15, 16
    physical defined, 16
Anthropology defined, 17
Archaeological consultation, 65
Archaeological remains, 28, 83–84, *see also* Native
        Americans
Archaeologist defined, 16
Area search, 11
Arsenic, 116, 117
Arthritic changes, 90, 132–133
Artifacts, 12
Autopsy, 9

B

Behavior of animals, *see* Animals
Bitemark analysis, 114–115
Blacks, sexual dimorphism in American,
    83
Blanching of bones, 100
Blood testing
    ABO typing, 115–116
    DNA, 116
Blunt trauma, 9, 123
Body, *see* Remains
Body changes, *see* Decomposition
Body position, *see* Disposition of body
Bone(s), *see also* Facial reconstruction;
        Skeletal remains
ancient versus modern, 73–77
bears' similarity to human, 72
blanching of, 100
burned, 63–65, 69
changes and time since death, 100
color and age of fracture, 128–129
duplication of, 78–79
femoral bowing, 74
femoral head
    for drug recovery, 117
    in sex determination, 85
femoral/humeral head diameter, in sex
    identification, 85
fetal, 72
field observations of, 60–61
fragmented, 70–72
human versus animal, 60–62, 70–73
hyoid and strangulation, 23–24, 78
infection of (osteomyelitis), 133–134
inventory of, 78, 139
juvenile, 60, 72
labeling of, 11
long, 60–61
    in sex identification, 85–86
    stature determination by, 92
of neonates, 72
versus non-bone, 69–71

165

osteon counting age determination technique, 113–114

pathologic changes in, 124–138, *see also* specific diseases

pelvic, in sex determination, 82–84

pubic symphysis, in age determination, 89–90

rib, 122, 124

samples taken from, 31

scattered, 12

skull, 70

   age determination by, 88–89

   blunt trauma to, 123

   deformation by coffin, 130

   in sex identification, 84–85

   vertebral, 131–132

Bone cysts, 138

Bone spurs, 137

Botanical consultation, 48–49, 140

Burial and decomposition, 100–101

Burial pits, 47–49, 57–58, *see also* Excavation

Burning, *see* Bones; Cremated remains

C

Cadavers, as facial reconstruction models, 108–109

Carbon dating, 74–75, 117

Case consolidation, 139–144

Case reports, 34–44

   examples

      complete adult skeleton, 36–40

      cremated remains, 40–42

      nearly complete remains, 42–44

   modification or clarification of, 35

   necessity for written, 35

   standarized forms for, 153–162

Caskets, *see* Coffins

Casting, permission for, 31

CAT scans

   of Egyptian mummies, 84

   as facial reconstruction database, 108–109

Cause of death, 141–142, 144

Cemetery practices, 53–55

Cervical (supernumerary) ribs, 134

Chain of evidence, 118

Children, *see* Juveniles

CIL (U.S. Army Central Identification Laboratory), *see* U.S. Army Central Identification Laboratories (CILs)

Civil War, 1, 2, 73–74

Climate, 8

Clothing, 60

   sex identification by, 81–82

   shoe print identification, 112–113

Coffins

   cemetery practices, 53–55

   decomposition and, 100–101

   deformation of body by, 116

Colorado, ancient remains statutes, 76–77

Commingled remains, 24–25, 60, 69–70, 78–79

Context, importance of, 29–30

Contract issues

   context, 29–30

   equipment, 30

   fees, 31–34

   informational, 29

   photography, 30–31

Craniofacial superimposition, 110–111

Cremated remains, 41, 64–65

"Crime of the Century" (O.J. Simpson trial), 118

D

Death

   cause of, *see* Cause of death

   time since, *see* Time since death

Decomposition, 7, 22–23, 61, 142

   of bone, 100

   burial and, 100–101

   insect development and, 101–102

   submersion and, 101

   and time of death, 99–100

   weather and, 100

Dental evidence, *see also* Teeth

   identification by, 40, 41, 74, 88, 89, 93–94, 139, 142

   time since death, 74–75

Dentition, *see* Teeth

Denver Museum of Natural History, 33, 130–131

Discovery phase

   defined, 19

   investigative approach following, 7–13, *see also* Recovery

Disease, ante-mortem, *see* Pathology

Dismemberment, 20–22, 123–124, *see also* Animals; Postmortem disturbance

Disposition of body, 140

   case report examples, 40, 41–42

Disturbance, post-mortem, *see* Dismemberment; Postmortem disturbance

DNA testing, 86, 116, 117–118

Documentation

   case reports, 34–44

   environmental categories of information, 102–103

   field recovery report, 66–67

   labeling of bones, 11

   skeletal pathology, 138

   standardized report form examples, 153–163

Dorsey, George, 2–3
Drug recovery, 117
Dwight, Dr. Thomas, 1, 2

E

Education
    academic, 26–27
    field experience, 27–28
Egyptian mummies, 83–84
Embalming, 99
Entomological consultation, *see* Insect evidence
Environmental categories of information,
        102–103
Epiphyseal bone spurs, 137
Epiphyseal growth, 72, 87
Ethnic identification, *see* Racial identification
Excavation, 57–60
Explosions, 69–70

F

Facial reconstruction, 105–112
    background and principles, 105–106
    cadavers as models, 108–109
    CAT scan and MRI data in, 109–110
    craniofacial superimposition, 110–111
    direct, 106–110
    museum versus forensic approach, 106
    University of Colorado Center for Human
        Simulation, 110
    University of Tenness*see* database, 109
    video superimposition, 112
Fees, 31–34
Femoral bowing, 74
Femoral head
    drug recovery from, 117
    in sex determination, 85
Fetal remains, 62, 72
Field examination, 60–65
Field experience as qualification, 27–28
Field Museum of Natural History (Chicago), 2–3
Field recovery, *see* Recovery
Flagging pin use, 52
Footprint impression analysis, 112–113
FORDISC software, 109
Forensic and medical terms, 147–152
Forensic anthropologist
    bias and premature information, 29
    contract issues
        equipment, 30
        fees, 31–34
        informational, 29
        photography, 30–31
    defined, 15, 16

educational requirements, 26–27
experience and credentials, 25–28
hiring issues
    context, 29–30
    interviewing of, 27–28
Forensic anthropology, historical development,
        1–5
Forensic odontology, 24, *see also* Dental evidence
Forensic toxicology, 115–117
Forms
    letters of agreement, 32, 33
    standardized report, 153–164
Fractures
    antemortem, 119–122
    in children, 120
    healed, 20, 21
    perimortem, 122–124
    postmortem, 122–124
    skull, 9
    spinal, 119, 121
    surgical prostheses in, 121
    ulnar parry, 122
Furue, Tadao, 5, 111

G

Glaister, John, 111
Glossary of terms, 147–152
Ground rules for investigation, 28–34
Growth centers of bone (epiphyses), 72, 87, 137
Gunshot wounds, 122–123, 126

H

Habitual activity, 133–134
Hair, 99–100, 115
Handedness, 38, 41, 95
Height, *see* Stature
Historical development of forensic anthropology,
        1–5
The Human Skeleton in Forensic Medicine
        (Krogman), 3
Humpback (kyphosis), 134
Hyoid bone and strangulation, 23–24, 78

I

Identification of the Human Skeleton (Dwight), 1
Individual characteristics
    dental, 40, 41, 74, 88, 89, 93–94
    handedness, 95
    pathology, 95
Infants
    bone differences in, 60, 62
    sex identification, 82

Insect evidence, 12, 140
    of time since death, 12, 74, 101–102,
        143–144
Interview criteria and process, 26–28
Investigation, ground rules for, 28–34
Investigative approach, 7–13
Investigative team, 10–11

J

Jewelry, 81
John Brown's body scenario, 7–13, 139–144
Juveniles
    bone differences in, 60, 62
    mass death of Vietnam orphans, 24–25
    sex identification, 82
    skull fractures in, 123

K

Kerley, Ellis, 4–5
Key questions and sequence, 69–96
    1: bone versus non-bone, 69–71
    2: human versus non-human remains, 71–73
    3: modern versus ancient remains, 73–77
    4: present and missing bones, 78
    5: single versus commingled remains,
        78–79
    6: race, ethnicity, and culture, 79–81
    7: sex, 81–86
    8: age, 86–91
    9: stature, 91–93
    10: individual characteristics, 93–95
Knife wounds, 122, 124, 125
Korean War, 4, 5
Krogman, Wilton Marion, 3, 5
Kyphosis (humpback), 134

L

Labeling, 11
Letters of agreement, 32, 33
Leutgert case, 3
Levitsky, Joseph, 117
Livor mortis, 98
Long bones, 60–61
    in sex identification, 85–86
    stature determination by, 92

M

Mass disasters, 24–25
Measurements, see Stature
Media hype, 105, 106, 113
Medical and forensic terms, 147–152

Metabolic diseases, 137
Missing persons records, 141
MRI scans, as facial reconstruction database,
    108–109
Mummification, 8, 83–84
Mutilated remains, see Animals; Dismembment;
    Postmortem disturbance

N

NAGPRA (Native American Graves Protection
    Act), 77–78
Native Americans, 74, 75–78, 130–131
Neonatal bones, 62, 72

O

Odors, 22, 53
O.J. Simpson trial, 118
Ossified thyroid cartilage, 23–24, 78
Osteologists, 16
Osteomyelitis, 133–134
Osteons (bone cells) in age determination,
    113–114
Osteoporosis, 134

P

Paleoserology (blood typing), 115–116
Parkman, Dr. George, 2
Parkman-Webster case, 2
Pathology (ante-and peri-mortem)
    arthritis, 21
    case report example, 39, 43
    case report examples, 43
    fracture, see Fractures
    individual identification by, 94–95
PCR (polymerase chain reaction), 118
Pelvic bones, in sex determination, 82–84
Perimortem trauma, 122–124
Photography, 143
    craniofacial superimposition, 110–111
    at discovery, 11
    before excavation, 57
    field recovery report, 67
    permission for, 30–31
    of vegetation, 57
Pickering, Robert, 5, 115
Plants, see Vegetation
Plastic with bone-like appearance, 70
Poisoning, 99–100, 116–117
Police records, 141
Polymerase chain reaction (PCR), 118
Postmortem disturbance, 23, 40, 41, 43, 63–65,
    123–128, see also Trauma

Postmortem trauma, 124–130
Prostheses, 121
Pseudotrauma, 130–131

Q

Qualifications
    academic, 26–27
    field experience, 27–28

R

Racial identification, 79–81
    case report examples, 37, 40, 42
    precedence over sex determination, 83
    skull characteristics, 80
    three-race model, 79–80
Radiography, see CAT scans; X-rays
Recovery
    by amateurs, 53–56, 142
    of clothing, 60
    defined, 19
    documentation and reporting, 66–67
    equipment for, 30–31, 45–46
    by forensic anthropologist, advantages of,
        10–13, 142–143
    fractures caused by, 128–129
    importance of completeness, 12
    importance of context, 29–30
    by law enforcement personnel, 8–10, 53–56,
        142
    observations, 46–50
        animal behavior or traces, 49–50
        archaeological consultation, 65
        bone type and condition, 60–61
        decomposition, 61–64
        disturbance or disguise, 63–65
        soil conditions, 47–49
    portion of remains, 53–56
    remains suspected to be present, 46–50
    second, 23
    techniques, 56–66
        examination, 60–65
        excavation, 57–60
Remains
    altered or disguised, 23
    archaeological, 28
    commingled, 24–25, 60, 69–70, 78–79
    conditions requiring examination, 17–19
    cremated, 41
    dating of, See Time since death
    decomposed, 7, 22–23, see also Decomposition
    discovery of, see Discovery
    dismembered or mutilated, 20–22, 123–124, see
        also Postmortem disturbance

fetal, 62
    moving/removal of, 9
    of neonates, 62, 72
    recovery of, see Recovery
    skeletal, 7, 11, see also Bone(s)
Report forms, standardized, 153–163
Reports, see Case reports; Documentation
Restriction fragment length polymorphism
        (RFLP), 118
Revere, Paul, 1–2
RFLP (restriction fragment length
        polymorphism), 118
Ribs
    cervical (supernumerary), 134
    injury to, 122, 124
Rigor mortis, 97–98
Robbins, Louise M., 112–113
Rodents, see Animals
Ruxton case (Scotland), 111

S

Scavengers, See Animals; Insect evidence
Schmorl's nodules, 133
Scoliosis, 134
Severed remains, see Dismemberment;
        Postmortem disturbance
Sex identification, 81–86
    case report examples, 37, 40, 42
    by clothing, 81–82
    by epiphyseal growth, 87
    by femoral/humeral head diameter, 85
    of juveniles, 82
    by long bones, 85–86
    by pelvic bones, 82–84
    by skull, 84–85
Sexual dimorphism, 83
Shoe print identification, 112–113
(O.J.) Simpson trial, 118
Skeletal Age in Young American Males (Kern &
        Stewart), 4
Skeletal remains, see Bone(s)
Skeletal trauma, see Trauma
Skull, 72, see also Facial reconstruction
    age determination by, 88–89
    blunt trauma to, 123
    deformation by coffin, 130
    fracture pattern in, 9–10
    racial characteristics of, 80
    in sex identification, 84–85
Snow, Dr. Charles, 4
Soil conditions, 47–49, 57–58, 100–101
Southeast Asians, sexual dimorphism in, 83
Stab wounds, 122, 124, 125
Standardized report form examples, 153–163

Stature, 91–93
    case report examples, 37–38, 40
Strangulation and hyoid bone, 23–24, 78
Submersion, 101
Surgical prostheses, 121

T

Taylor, President Zachary, 99–100, 116
Teeth, *see also* Dental evidence
    age determination by, 88
    bitemark analysis, 114–115
    case report examples, 40, 41
    growth chronology, 88, 89
    individual characteristics of, 93–94
    Native American shovel-shaped incisors,
        74
Temperature loss, 98
(University of) Tennes*see* facial reconstruction
        database, 108–109
Terminology, 147–152
Thyroid cartilage, ossified, 23–24, 78
Time since death, 35, 42, 73–77, 142, 143–144,
        see also Decomposition
    algor mortis and, 98
    artifactual evidence, 74
    body condition and, 99–100
    bone evidence, 73–74
    carbon dating, 117
    clothing as evidence, 74
    dental evidence, 74–75
    embalming effects on estimation, 99
    insect evidence, 12, 74, 101–102, 143–144
    livor mortis and, 98
    microenvironment and, 100–102
    principles of estimating, 97–98
    rigor mortis and, 97–98
Todd, T.W., 3
Toxicology, 116–117
    President Zachary Taylor case, 99–100,
        116
Trauma
    antemortem, 38, 42, 43, 119–122
    blunt, 9, 123
    perimortem, 38–39, 42, 43, 122–124
    postmortem, 40, 124–130
    pseudo-, 130–131
    reporting protocol, 35
    severe, 24–25
Trotter, Dr. Mildred, 4

Tucker, Lt. Colonel, 35
Tumors, 137

U

University of Tennes*see* facial reconstruction
        database, 108–109
U.S. Army Central Identification Laboratories
        (CILs), 3–4
    Hawaii, 4, 5, 111
    Japan, 111
    Thailand, 4–5, 24–25

V

Vegetation, 48–49, 140
    photography of, 57
    time since death and, 101
    volunteer, 48–49
Vertebrae, 133
Vertebral disks, 134
Vietnam War, 4–5, 79, 115

W

WAG (wild-assed guess) principle, 93
Warren, Charles F., 4–5
Warren, Charles P., 24–25
Warren, Dr. Joseph, 1–2
Weather, 100
Webster, Dr. John White, 2
Webster-Parkman case, 2
Weight, 92–93
Wildlife officers, 140, 143
World War II, 3–4, 5, 47

X

X-rays
    of antemortem fractures, 119–120
    antemortem medical, 94, 95
    of arthritic changes, 132–133
    dental, 88
    of Egyptian mummies, 84
    postmortem, 9

Y

Yada, Dr. Shoichi, 115
Yap Island case, 47, 100–101